SPONGEHEADZ: U & MEdia

Stay tuned

Lynn Ziegler

LYNN ZIEGLER

BOOK PUBLISHERS NETWORK

Book Publishers Network
P.O. Box 2256
Bothell • WA • 98041
Ph • 425-483-3040

10 9 8 7 6 5 4 3 2

Printed in the United States of America

LCCN 2006933635

ISBN 1-887542-44-2

Editor: Vicki McCown

Cover Design: Travis Milberger

Interior Layout: Stephanie Martindale

Cover Photography: Cindy Ho

Sponges: John Engerman

DEDICATION

To Peggy Charren, Woman Warrior of the Airwaves, who inspired my work in this field and who, despite her protestations, will always be my "cosmic godmother"—

To my mom, Rosemary O'Keefe Ziegler, who gave me my love for wordplay and language, and my father, Walter Richard Ziegler, who taught me to love and respect the waves—

And to my extraordinary children—my son, Christopher, my daughter, Jesse, and my son, Alik Aaglupak Crockett, who spent thirty-nine years of their collective childhoods living with this project: I treasure your faith in me and your ability to keep me going in challenging times. Thank you for your love and laughter. You are part of every page and every breath.

I love you.

The final dedication is on the last page of this book.

LZ

TABLE OF CONTENTS

THE BUTTONS (and how to push them)

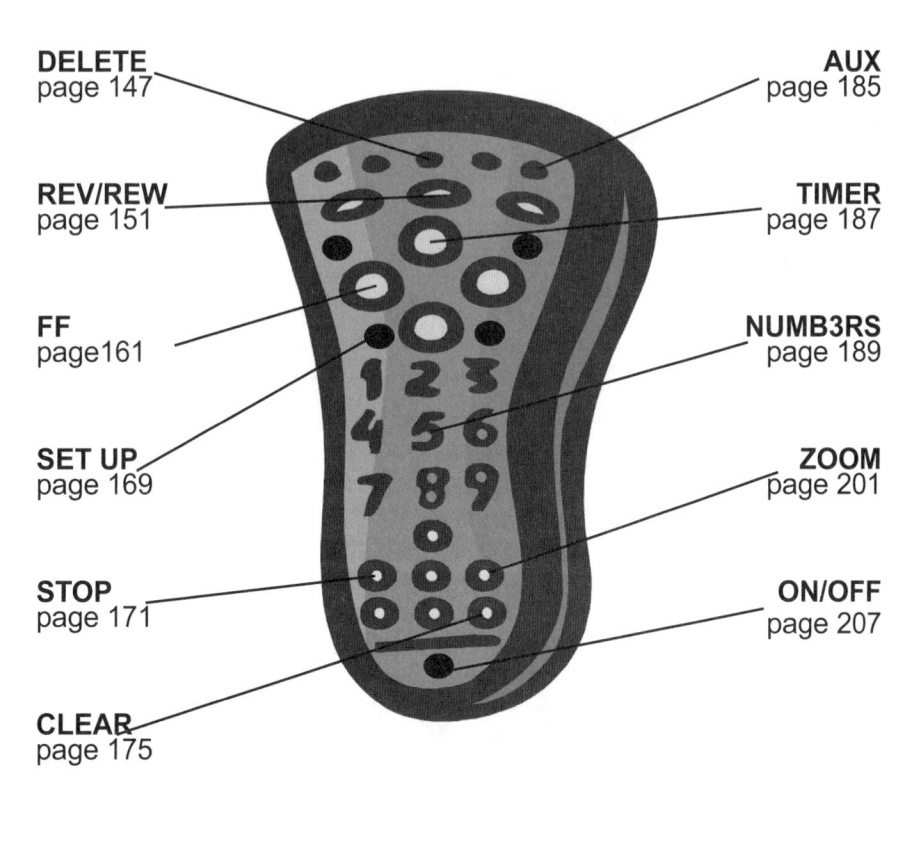

DELETE
page 147

AUX
page 185

REV/REW
page 151

TIMER
page 187

FF
page161

NUMB3RS
page 189

SET UP
page 169

ZOOM
page 201

STOP
page 171

ON/OFF
page 207

CLEAR
page 175

FOREWORD

How different the world would be if parents began to view their children as "Spongeheadz." No longer would we be able to consider the time a child spends in front of a "screen" as simply "entertainment." If we imagine the child's impressionable young mind as eagerly absorbing all of the content laid so generously before him/her in this huge cafeteria of choices, we may find ourselves wanting to take a critical second look at the ways in which our children are spending their time.

Media scholar and pioneer researcher George Gerbner frequently used to point out to his audiences the important role that storytelling has played in ensuring that our culture has been passed down through the generations. Our most cherished, institutions, including the family, the school, our faith-based organizations, and our communities, have played key roles in ensuring that these stories are passed successfully to our young. There are now, however, newer and much more powerful storytellers that threaten to surpass all our institutions in their storytelling capabilities.

SPONGEHEADZ: U & MEdia

These new storytellers are, of course, the TV and other screen media. We, as parents, need to be ever-cognizant of the stories that our children are hearing/viewing about our world each and every day.

While there are those who would maintain that the issue of what our children are absorbing can simply be addressed by "turning off" the TV in the home, new technologies continually challenge the validity of that argument. Video programming is now even more accessible by many other means beyond the TV screen. If your child has access to a computer, a cell phone, and/or a video iPod or PDVR (to name a few), new video is only a click away.

According to a recent report by the Kaiser Family Foundation (2005), there is little doubt that young people today live media-saturated lives, spending an average of nearly six and a half hours a day with media. Kaiser concludes that across the seven days of the week, *that amount is equivalent to a full-time job, with a few extra hours thrown in for overtime!* An additional factor to consider here is that while many of these young people are using media, they may actually be involved with more than one medium at a time (e.g., listening to music, reading, **and** instant-messaging friends). These young people are clearly packing their six and a half hours a day with all kinds of media exposure!

Spongeheadz absorb all screen content; we can no longer assume that all of this content is being absorbed without having some impact. Just as our children learn to turn the pages in a book without ever really understanding all of the words it contains, so also are they learning to access a wide variety of media without necessarily having developed all of the critical thinking skills that they will need to "read" all of these new texts. Critical thinking and problem solving should no longer be confined only to tasks involving the printed word; our texts have moved far beyond the printed word. The media powerfully present their messages, and these messages require the development of critical viewing skills.

So, what's a parent to do? This important book is filled with suggestions as to how you can begin taking action in your own home. Author Lynn Ziegler, children's media critic and parent of three children, understands the constant demands on all of us. She understands the misplaced temptation to just "let the TV do some babysitting for a while." It is in this spirit that she offers ideas that she and other parents have tested in their own homes. Her easy-to-read and entertaining approach to her subject matter makes it possible to sandwich in time to read her book while immersed in the hectic daily routine of parenting. Yet each chapter contains a wealth of valuable information. *Spongeheadz: U & MEdia* is a must-read for all of us trying to raise children in this media-saturated world!

Marilyn Cohen, Ph.D.
Director
NW Center for Excellence in Media Literacy
College of Education, University of Washington
Seattle, WA
Action for Media Education, Founder and Executive Director

ACKNOWLEDGMENTS

The book you hold in your hands could not have been possible without the support and assistance of my family and friends.

Special thanks to Connie Sullivan, Bill Ballard, Laurie Sorensen and Carroll L Bryan II, and Marilyn Bierman. Thanks to Chris Power, Diana Ferris Cotter, Sarah Moores, Sara Meitner (Germany), Wende, Richard and Aiden Jowsey (NZ), Lee Burton (AUS), Peter Clayton (UK and Canada), Marilyn Cohen, Barbara Johnson and the people of AME, Dr. Susan Linn, Dr. Alvin Poussaint, Diane Levin, Jean Kilbourne, Nancy Carlsson-Paige, Frank Baker, Robert Mc Chesney, and especially Rob Williams and Sara Voorhees of ACME for their generous support and encouragement to finish this book.

To Jean Tosh, Dao Ho, Robin Anderson, Kathleen Winters, Keith Riggs, Michael and Kathy Hodecker, Mary Gorichanaz, Lori Lupo, Chris the Post Office Wizard, Dawn and Peter Lounsbury, Carol and Leah Thurston, and Leah's brother Josh, my late and inspiring student (now snowboarding in the afterlife.) Your friendship is treasured, and you kept SPONGEHEADZ (and me) afloat.

Many thanks to Linda Ellerbee for her encouragement, her wickedly delicious sense of humor, for teaching me to forge on, and for celebrating this mantra: "IF YOU WANNA KNOW, ASK!" This book would not have been possible without you.

And thanks to two other parts of the Texan Trinity: Molly Ivins, who inspires me with every column, and Ann Richards, who knew a thang or three about turning a phrase—you will be missed. And NYT's MoDo—redhead 2 redhead, you keep me fired up.

Thanks to Norman Lear, Bill Moyers, Christiane Amanpour, Maria Hinojosa, Anderson Cooper, Keith Olbermann, Seattle's own "Mediatrician" Don Schifrin, M.D. (past President of the American Academy of Pediatrics, who has been prescribing media literacy for years!) and many others whose works inspire me, and who bring excellence to TV and all media.

Thanks to Amy Goodman and the folks at Democracy Now!, Women's eNews, Free Press, Creative Voices, Commercial Alert, Josh Golin at CCFC, and all the organizations who work on media literacy issues, and who shared their time, their research, and their stories with me, and to Mark Morford of **www.sfgate.com**, for raising wordplay to an art form, especially when it's seasoned with impossible stylistic synergy and good giggles.

Boundless gratitude to Oprah Winfrey for celebrating reading and for putting books in the hands of adults and children all over the world. A decade into this book, you turned to a guest on set (talking about kids and TV) and said, "Children are spongeheads, aren't they?" I knew you got it (and you get it!) After the shock of hearing my title come out of your mouth, I picked myself up off the floor, and I redoubled my efforts to finish this work. In your honor, the first quote in this book is by Maya Angelou, whose gifts, like yours, are oceanic and immeasurable.

Thank you, also, for making it possible to bring four of my Native American women GED students to attend the Seattle "Live Your Best Life" event. Sharing space and time with you was/is life-changing. Ever since I heard you read it in person many years ago, you've defined "Phenomenal Woman" for me.

Lynn Ziegler

Thanks to J.K. Rowling for her inspiration to a writing single mother, and for demonstrating that there is a certain magic to every book (even nonfiction ones!) And thanks to the many, many others whose work fires my imagination.

Thanks to President William Jefferson Clinton for his encouragement on this project, and for all he is doing for children around the planet, especially in the fight against pediatric AIDS and in post-tsunami recovery efforts. Your good works show kids the dynamic power of compassion; thanks for celebrating diversity and children in media, as you always have. You inspired me to donate a portion of the sale of every copy of this book to UNICEF (for tsunami children) and, along with Oprah Winfrey, to replace books in children's libraries in the Gulf Coast states and in Africa.

To Senator Hillary Rodham Clinton: Thanks for helping people realize that it takes an electronic village to heal from heartache. Your work for this nation's children, especially the children of military families and 9/11 survivors, has been simply stellar. Your greatest work is still ahead of you. I am the daughter of native New Yorkers—even though I now live in the only state with two female senators and a woman governor (Washington State, well-represented by Senators Maria Cantwell and Patti Murray and Governor Chris Gregoire). I consider myself one of your constituents as well.

Thanks to Pat Schroeder, Michael Jacobsen of the Centers for Science in the Public Interest (CSPI), and to the First Consumer Advocate: Ralph Nader. When I interviewed you years ago, you said that someone "ought to write a book for kids on media." I told you, "I'm working on it." Here it is.

Thanks to Al Gore for Current TV's VC2, "viewer-created content," and for bringing us a second "inconvenient truth" with grace and courage.

Thank you to the musicians and songwriters whose work kept me company while I sang and wrote (sometimes simultaneously) particularly the Beatles, the Eagles, Bonnie Raitt, Jackson Browne, Stevie Wonder, Sting, Alicia Keys, to Mimi for "Make It Happen" (I did!) and to my late friend, Laura Nyro.

SPONGEHEADZ: U & MEdia

A special debt of gratitude to the Native American families whose feedback and suggestions are interwoven throughout this book, and in particular to Barbara Lawrence, M.Ed., of the Suquamish Tribe, and our mutual mentor, the late (and awesome!) Marion Forsman-Boushie. To Judge Mary Pearson at the Colville Nation, and vice-presidential candidate Winona LaDuke: Thanks for reminding us all that strong women can do anything. To my tribal students and their children, thank you for your energy and your generosity.

Thanks to Wayne, Judy, Ryan Ziegler, Gary Ziegler, Anne Hopkins, and to my childhood BFF, Jeanne Hopkins Koch, who still managed to ask, after forty-five years of friendship and thirteen years on this project, "Book? You're writing a book?!"

Thanks to Cindy Ho, who took the cover photo of elementary school kids (and the author's backcover pic), and to the team who worked on putting this book together, particularly Sheryn, Steph, Travis, and Vicki. John Engerman gets a squeeze for donating a sponge.

Thanks to John Callahan, whose work keeps me (and Robin Williams, Gary Larsen, and Kinky Friedman, among others) laughing, for donating his cartoons for this book. This is how we roll, John!

Thanks to J.S., for four decades of intuitive inspiration.

Gratitude to the Animalia chez nous. And all the dog and cat hair. And purrs and smiles.

Finally, thanks to S.B. for holding my face and my heart in your hands.

Be well—and enjoy!

LZ

INTRODUCTION

That thing on top of your child's neck is a giant sponge.

Our kids are "spongeheadz"—absorbing whatever they see and hear on screen. Because our kids soak up so much, so fast, it's in everyone's best interest to make certain that what they're absorbing is, to quote a Tina Turner song, "simply the best." As tempting as it may be, we can't dismiss TV as "garbage in, garbage out." If that's your expectation, you won't be disappointed.

Kids deserve better.

In fact, the last thing anyone, particularly a child, needs to be is a passive viewer. The first step out of whatever you believe is the primordial airwave slime is to become an activist media consumer—a critical thinker. Contrary to popular belief (and most books about media), there IS wonderful stuff on TV. But to find it, we need to change how we look at what we watch.

Think: "SMART IN, SMARTER OUT." If our kids can "read" media (SMART IN), they'll be more objective and more critical as they watch, and will benefit (SMARTER OUT) from **any** viewing time. They'll go into each media experience better informed and positioned to make smarter choices. And those critical thinking skills carry over into nearly every part of a kid's life.

Being a couch potato (or any other veggie) is a luxury we can no longer afford. "Enhanced TV" and interactive viewing experiences are already part of daily life, and even more a part of our children's lives than our own. Children see something on TV, and then go to a Web site, like NOGGIN's "**www.the-n.com**." Or, they may find a Web site promoting a high-interest show, like **www.scifinetwork.com**, and then tune in. We can transition into this new kind of viewing with a how-to manual that keeps our focus where it belongs: tuning in to the kind of programming that helps children lead healthy and productive lives, celebrating curiosity and learning as they do so.

So welcome to media literacy. It's as important as any other kind of reading—numerical, grammatical, or techno/computer. It has been required coursework for more than two decades in nearly every industrialized, developed nation (Great Britain, Japan, Germany, France, Canada, Australia, New Zealand) except one—the one that produces most of the programming and commercials: OURS. Fortunately, this is changing, and now, you can be part of that change.

Media literacy is more than recognizing that you are a media consumer. It's understanding your responsibilities as a citizen and **reclaiming the airwaves that are rightfully yours.**

> **Nothing will work unless you do.**
> Maya Angelou, Poet, Peacemaker, Activist

In the "Resources" portion of this book, you'll find some wonderful organizations promoting media literacy and weaving it into all kinds of learning. These sites not only offer information and activities, but many make available free learning packets and lesson plans for teachers. All of the organizations in "Resources" have been personally screened, and the best of the best appear there. Let's hope this list continues to grow.

The next time you turn on the TV, keep in mind these five tips from *Better Viewing Magazine:*

TV has a point of view. Challenge it.

TV isn't real life. Spot the illusions.

TV manipulates. Identify its techniques—and your reactions to them.

TV is limited. Guess what was left out.

TV is a business. Understand your economic role—and your power—AS A VIEWER.

So, no matter what your neighbor with the "KILL YOUR TELEVISION" bumper sticker says, **THERE IS GOOD STUFF OUT THERE**. Consider the "remote" possibility of getting something out of TV watching besides a series of screen changes, measured as unproductive time. Your viewing experiences can be, as the Arts and Entertainment Network (A & E) is so fond of telling us, "time well spent."

HOW TO USE THIS BOOK

SPONGEHEADZ: U & MEdia is designed to raise a lot more questions than it answers.

The framework of *SPONGEHEADZ: U & MEdia* is that time-honored piece of Americana, that device that has launched more wrestling matches than the WWE: yes, The Remote. No matter what name it goes by in your house, (Clicker, Zapper, R.C., The Thingy, "THAT," etc.), it is the handheld conflict facilitator in the nightly onscreen-in-the-living-room turf war. In 2006, it turned fifty years old.

Let's face it: If you consider the way we use the remote control, it only needs two buttons, and here they are:

NEXT ! and WHAT WAS THAT?
GO BACK!

Call it the basic viewer's mantra—unless, of course, the brain gets into the game. (See the VIEW button.)

What you hold in your hands—this book—is a different kind of remote control. These buttons will do more than change channels—they will change your way of thinking. Instead of being powered by batteries, this remote is powered by grey matter—yours and your children's.

We can't change what we've seen on TV. But we can change how we look at what we see.

SPONGEHEADZ: U & MEdia takes the remote and changes the meanings of all the buttons.

For example, the chapter named for the SELECT button is about advertising aimed at children. After all, SELECT is the command that underlies every televised commercial. We are offered the chance, the opportunity (often for a limited time only!) to SELECT a certain product that we've become convinced we need, and to purchase one brand over another, because the SELECTed brand will make us (choose any or all of the following) thinner, cooler, wealthier, smarter, sexier, healthier, more athletic, more attractive, more desirable, more prestigious, more accessible, more influential, and, in a few cases, more informed.

You get the picture.

And so do our kids, who see three thousand advertising messages a day, a number that's going to rise exponentially in 2006 and beyond, as cell phones and podcasts evolve as new playgrounds for marketers.

"Three thousand a day? No way," parents say to me. Then I remind them that most kids have seen or heard hundreds of ads (TV and radio commercials at home, in the car, on the bus, in newspapers, magazines, signage on buildings and vehicles, pop-ups on the computer) before they've even picked up a pencil at school (assuming that they are still using pencils there, or after all the funding cuts, that your school system can still afford to provide them.)

Some other examples of rethinking the buttons: The **COLOR** button is about diversity and its importance to children. The **STEREO(types)** our kids see and hear can form lasting (and erroneous) opinions—a good reason to start those tolerance discussions as early as possible. What defines your family's comfort zone in terms of onscreen behavior and presentation? Maybe you'll find out when you see what's on **DISPLAY**. **PAUSE** buttons are interspersed for humor and feature the terrific work of cartoonist John Callahan. And so on.

At the end of every chapter, parents can **ZAP!** home the point of each button (chapter) with some simple and inexpensive activities. Some of them are short enough to be done during a commercial break—others will take more time. They've been "kid-tested, parent-approved." Following these suggestions will, I hope, make TV watching more of an active, shared experience than a passive assault on your senses—and your wallet!

Scattered throughout the text are remotes designed by elementary school children from a rainbow of Pacific Northwest communities—kids of as many colors, backgrounds, ethnicities, and genetic blends as possible. I am proud to say that *SPONGEHEADZ: U & MEdia* is the product of more influence from Native American children and their families than any previous book on kids and television.

You will notice sea-sponge-shaped blobs appearing within these pages. These contain quotes and observations from real kids and other Very Important People.

You've ruined TV for me. Now I hafta think—thanks a lot!
An anonymous student, following a media literacy presentation in Seattle (and smiling)

TV has been interactive from the start. It makes us laugh. It makes us cry. It has become an ever-more-intrusive window on the globe, including parts of the planetary backdrop that we thought (or hoped) we could avoid.

It brings us the world.

At its best, TV can show the power and compassion of the people on this planet, who can, in the midst of dramatic world events, reach out and initiate acts of improbable strength and unfathomable kindness.

It's a kaleidoscope, vividly colored and impossibly complex.

It's the cobalt electronic hearth.

Can it still inspire us to think? We can hope so.

After all, we are all SPONGEHEADZ.

PLAY

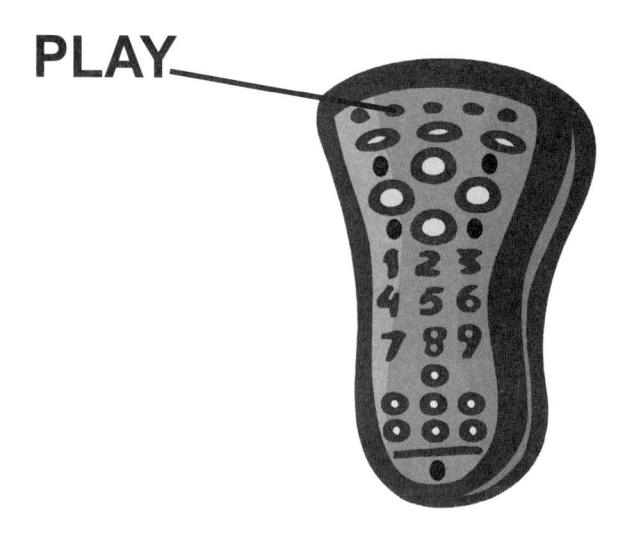

Follow the instructions on any piece of electronics, and

JUST PUSH PLAY.

Before your child sits down to watch TV, make an effort to choose that activity as a last (*not* the first!) option.

PUSHING PLAY is one way we can all put the brakes on this country's childhood obesity problem. You and your child can make a list of all the reasons your offspring can't "go out and play." (You can have fun with this.)

For example:

✗ It's dark. (Or it's raining, snowing, too hot, too cold, Hurricane Zeta is on its way.)

✗ We live in an apartment with no play area except the street.

✗ We live on a street where there's no one to play with.

✗ There are kids to play with, but none of them like me.

✗ There are kids to play with, but I don't like any of them.

✘ None of the things I want to play with have been invented yet.

✘ I don't want to be abducted by aliens, pirates, or superheroes. (Or, on a serious note, anybody else, either.)

AND THE WORST ONE:

✘ I'M BORED.

Encourage your kid to make up the loopiest reasons to watch TV, and pull out all the stops. Then, after you've had a good laugh…

…Make a list (together, if possible) of things your child can play with that don't involve sitting and staring. Yes, that leaves out other forms of screen time, like video or computer games.

It does include:

☆ Listening to music

☆ Dancing

☆ Painting or engaging in all kinds of arts and crafts, like quilting, knitting, building

☆ Exercising (stretches for sports, easy reps of some sort of motion)

☆ Creating your own entertainment (writing a comic book, making a video, trying claymation or developing wildly improbable storyboards, creating and recording a radio program with original sound effects)

☆ Taking pictures (Yes, let them borrow your new phone, if necessary.)

☆ Organizing (their stuff, your stuff, stuff to recycle or donate)

☆ Participating in a community activity for the greater good

☆ Walking

☆ Playing cards (Blackjack and rummy teach math skills and pattern recognition.)

☆ Playing board games, including chess, checkers, and backgammon…all involve strategy

☆ Playing Scrabble or trivia games, WHICH ALL INCLUDE READING!

☆ Going to the library and bringing back a stack of high-interest books chosen by your kid, because even if you have books stacked to the ceiling in your home, NONE OF THEM WILL BE INTERESTING ANYMORE.

Another good goal: NO CHILD LEFT INSIDE!

Then, if all else fails, watch TV—but only if you agree to THINK ABOUT WHAT YOU'RE WATCHING AND WHY.

**AP**

1. Take a huge sheet of recycled paper and some crayons, and design a community media center.

2. Flip the paper over, and design the TV of the future. Then visit **www.howtoons.com**, a site that turns kids into inventors by celebrating what the site founder, Dr. Saul Griffith, calls children's "physical intuition" for understanding science and creativity.

3. Take this book outside and read it to your kids while you're checking to see if the water's rising (yet).

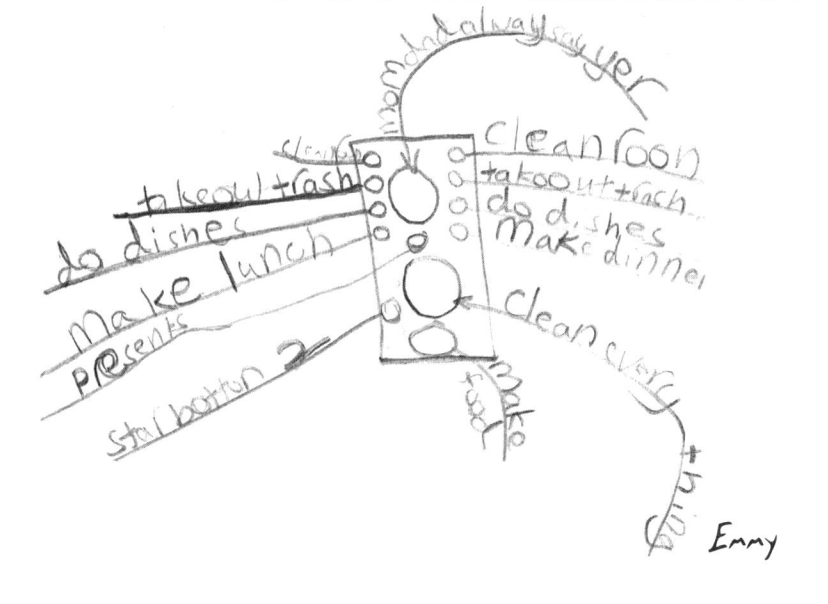

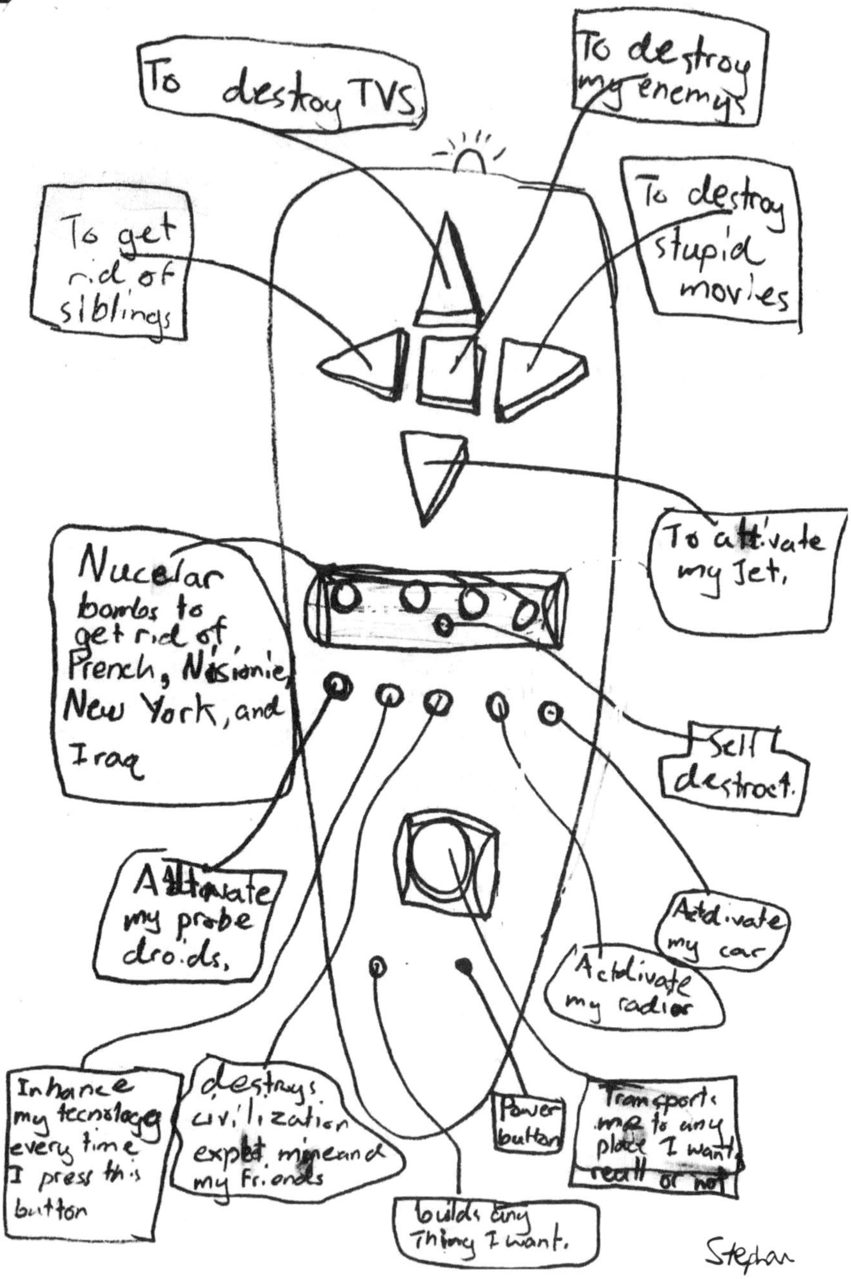

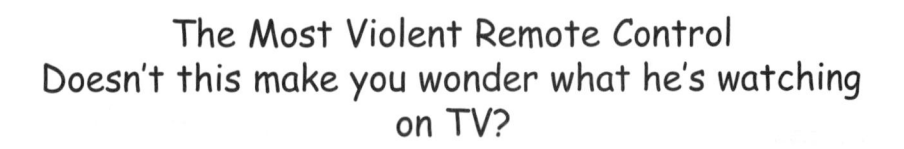

The Most Violent Remote Control
Doesn't this make you wonder what he's watching on TV?

MUTE

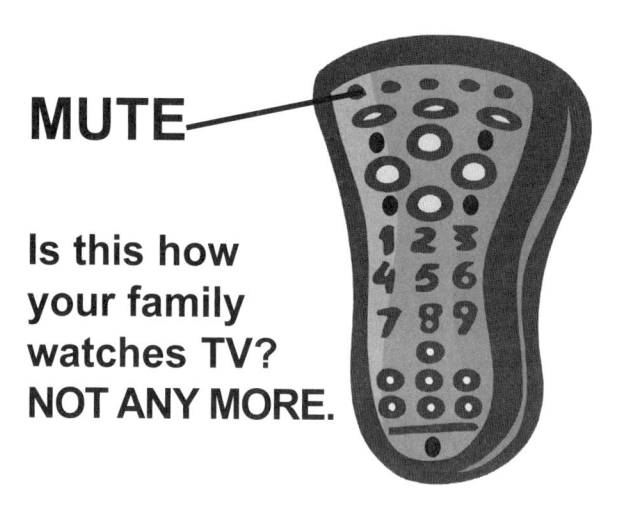

Is this how
your family
watches TV?
NOT ANY MORE.

Linda Ellerbee has often been heard to say, "You are smarter than your TV," and it's true.

Then why do so many of us sit silently and absorb what's on without talking back?

SO PUSH THE MUTE BUTTON.

Start out slowly. Don't decide to explore your first "mute-tation" experience during a season finale, the end of a mini-series, or a major live sporting event (especially any listing including the word "playoffs.") Instead, pick a rerun of a live-action program that your kids have seen at least once before (but can't yet recite verbatim.)

Let your collective eyeballs zero in on the screen.

What does the picture tell you?

What does the cast look like? Are they all the same age? Color? Size? Ethnicity? Ability? Class? Gender? What does their body language tell you about the story line, and how do gestures and expressions move the plot along? What's the setting in time and space, and how can you tell?

Admittedly, there may be some outcries. "DO YOU *MIND*?" is one of the more acceptable responses you may hear, and you can actually use it—your mind, that is. Urging the other people in the room to use theirs (before they find the remote and turn the sound back on!), break down the word MUTE, and do it fast:

> **M**ind. That's exactly the point. We're going to use yours and pay attention in a different way, without sound for a while.
>
> **U**nhook from other activities.
>
> **T**alk. To each other—and the TV.
>
> **E**valuate what you've seen and "understood."

Even if you only do this for one segment, or until the first commercial break, kids will instantly realize that dialogue isn't the only missing element. The laugh track is gone. So is the music, if there was any. (So will any references to named products on the set—more of that when we push the SELECT button.)

See how easy that was? You have just stuck your toe into the (air)waves and tried out critical thinking. Of course, within seconds, your inner voice might start screeching, "OK. Big deal. That works with sitcoms. I can't talk back to other shows." Of course you can. *Talkback Live* is not just the name of a once-upon-CNN talk show; it is a great first step in critical thinking and a valuable viewer's mantra.

Here are some examples of ways to talk back to your TV. This is by no means a complete list—just a mental launching pad for the idea.

> The best thing about TV is
> that it can be educational.
> The worst thing is that TV can also rot
> your brain!
> Trevor, grade 6

TALKBACK 2 SPORTS - Sports fanatics can proudly say they've been talking to the TV as long as it's been plugged in. Was that last call fair? If your opinion was different, did the instant replay change it—or confirm it?

TALKBACK 2 COURT SHOWS - Did you side with the petitioner, the defendant, or Judge Judy/Mablean/Milian/Hatchett/Mills/Brown/Alex et al? Was justice served? How do you know? Want to argue the point? If you don't want to watch broadcast court shows, remember that Court TV is a cable network of its own, and there are stations where you can catch *Law and Order* (and any of its offspring) 24/7. Many of the plotlines claim to be "ripped from the headlines." Then you can hash the verdicts to death (ad nauseam) on discussion panels from Nancy Grace to Larry King. Never discourage a child from arguing his or her point—you may have a budding attorney in the family.

Sara

TALKBACK 2 SITCOMS - Whatever the dilemma is, it's solved in twenty-two minutes. How realistic is that? Is that how your family works things out? As sitcoms tackle more and more difficult social issues, such as eating disorders, tobacco/alcohol/substance abuse, sexuality, values and choices, and change, it's even MORE critical to jump-start a discussion.

TALKBACK 2 DRAMA - Is there a real ending? Is there a cliffhanger? (This is a given at the end of a season or during "sweeps," which are ratings periods, but it's used more often than that.) Sometimes, the most annoying ending is one that reads "to be continued" (especially if the promos for the show have minimized that fact. They have to tell you—but HOW they tell you is sometimes fuzzy.) Would you have ended the show a different way?

TALKBACK 2 CARTOONS - Cartoons are different in the post-millenial world. While they have improved somewhat in diversity, they have plummeted in terms of what used to be called "good taste." Case in point: *Drawn Together*, which bills itself as the "first animated reality-TV show," makes *South Park* look like Disney. Or *Ren and Stimpy*, who used to discuss almost daily why dogs look at catboxes as a venue for interesting snack options. There's a big EEEEEWWW factor.

The discerning parent has two choices: BLAME the show in question and be offended, and confirm your kid's growing assumption that you are so, like, "out of it." (See the last four letters of "BLAME.") Or, you can say, "That's really gross! What do you think gave the animators an idea like that?" This dissolves the ICK factor and reminds the child that someone actually wrote the script and drew the pictures (and sent them off to an Asian animation studio.) Ask your kid, "And what could you have drawn there that would have been funnier?"

TALKBACK 2 NEWS - An entire chapter of this book (optimistically entitled **BALANCE,** in a satirical nod to a network that is anything but) will discuss news in detail. The important thing is first to talk back—and question what you're hearing and seeing, particularly if you hold a different viewpoint on the story. Always ask, **"WHAT'S MISSING?"**

TALKBACK 2 COMMERCIALS (AND POLITICAL ADS!) - The short version of this is **"QUESTION EVERYTHING."** The longer versions will be discussed in the chapters **SELECT** and **ZOOM.** Commercials, whether for people or potato chips, are asking you for your money. Make certain that you know what you're being sold.

ZAP 1. Try "reading" a show on closed-captioning out loud. Hesitant readers may enjoy being able to deliver simple lines of dialogue, even if they only do one character at a time. (Be sure to pick a familiar, live action show whose characters and pacing your child may already know.) Then, move on to fresh material.

2. Choose an animated show and try the same thing. How did the artist exaggerate the facial expressions of the character to make a point?

3. Watch and record a "simulcast" event (radio coverage with TV pictures). Was there any difference between the TV version and the one that the radio station offered?

Keep a spiral notebook and a pen somewhere near the remote control. Decorate it with drawings and doodles of "TV stuff." In fact, feel free to do that in any blank pages of this book.

Take—and MAKE notes! The whole family can use these "jottings." When the book/pad/spiral is filled in a few months (or, better, plan to change it by season), you may be surprised at what's in it. If you see something on TV that's really terrific (or at the other end of the spectrum), write down the channel, date, and time you watched it. Then, at the end of the night or weekend (or month or season), write a letter or e-mail to the station that broadcast one of those programs.

**UNLESS YOU'RE A MIME,
MUTE IS NOT CUTE.**

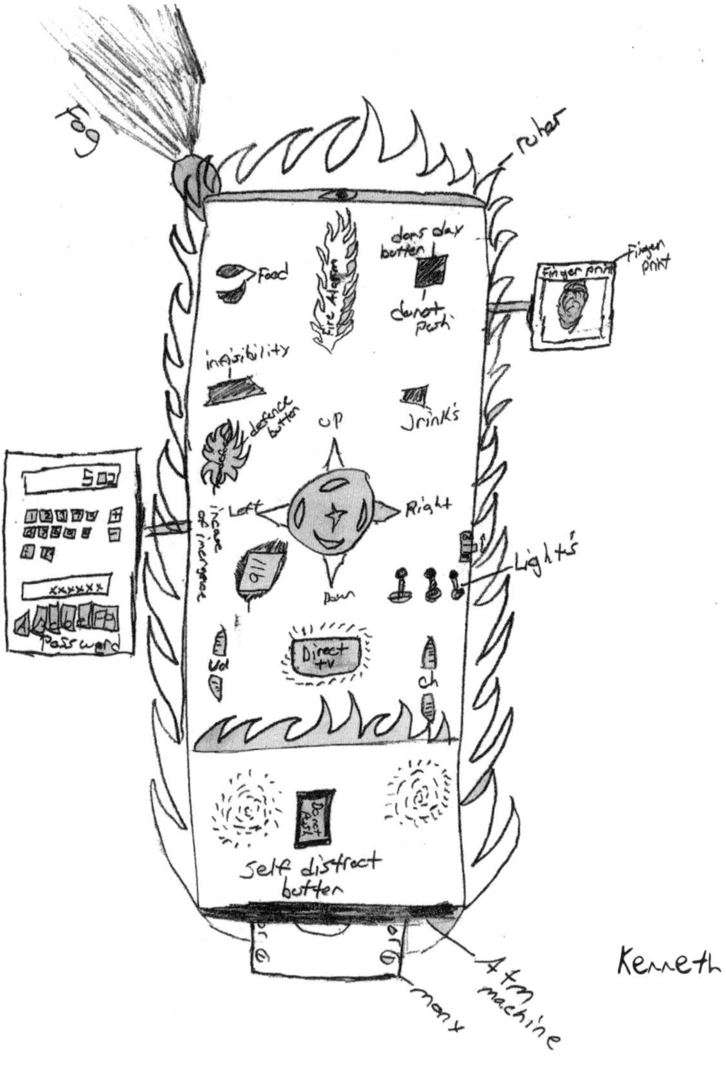

Fog

rotar

Food

fire alarm

dans dax button

danart posh

finger print

Finger Print

invisibility

defence button

Drinks

increase of insurgent

UP

Left

Right

Down

Lights

116

Password

Vol

Direct tv

ch

self distract button

A tm machine

man x

Kenneth

VIEW

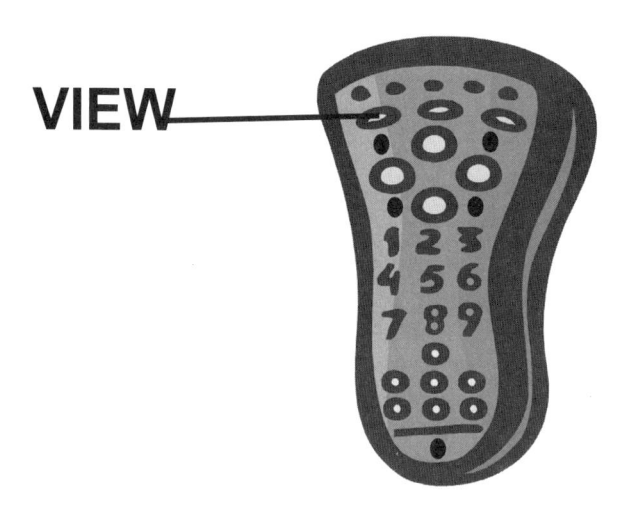

1 2 3
4 5 6
7 8 9

We all know that we "watch" TV. But few people understand how we actually see it.

Have you ever heard of David Letterman's "Stupid Pet Tricks?" Have you ever watched a reality show that features "Stupid Human Tricks?" Of course you have. And in either case, part of the entertainment value is that you never know what's really going to happen. (Having seen both, I recommend you bet on the pet, as some "Stupid Human Tricks," like eating cockroaches or being covered in spiders or scorpions or worse, simply defy comprehension, even when big advertising dollars are involved. So much for *Fear Factor* and its slimy spinoffs!)

Watching TV is not a "Stupid Human Trick." What's going on behind your eyes is pretty remarkable. Thanks to the visionaries at **www.howstuffworks.com** for highlighting these points—think of these as "Cool Brain Moves."

<u>**COOL BRAIN MOVE NUMBER ONE**</u>: **If a still image is divided into a collection of very small dots, your brain will reassemble those dots into a meaningful image.**

<u>**COOL BRAIN MOVE "PART DEUX"**</u>: **If a moving scene is divided into a sequence of still pictures, and these images are shown**

in rapid succession, your brain will reassemble those still images into a single, moving picture.

By now you may be saying, "Deux? How about DUH?"

You've learned enough about images to understand that the "fusion of small dots" tricks are used everywhere—TVs, computers, monitors. On screens, these are called pixels. The more there are, the more defined is the picture, which is why so many people are looking forward to the changeover from analog TV to digital HDTV—high definition television.

"Cool Brain Move Part Deux" is simply the art of the flip book, the way every kid first grasps animation. A succession of 15 still images per second looks like fluid movement—fewer than that makes the images jumpy. Flashing 24 frames per second is infinitely smoother—that's how we view film. TV is broadcast at 30 frames per second. Interestingly enough, our brains process those frames at a max of about 8 per second—which means you and your spongeheadz are not registering all that you see. And that's OK.

The really astonishing thing is that our brains do these two Cool Moves simultaneously. Behind the frontal lobes of our Spongeheadz is a mini-studio, mixing sound and visuals, before we even get to comprehending the content.

As long as we're looking at how we see the big picture, check out some of the new additions to the screen itself. The lower third of your screen (where you probably are already used to seeing a moving line of printed breaking news, storm warnings, and election results, called "crawls") has become a much busier place than ever before, with occasionally (and accidentally) comic results.

Thanks to ever-evolving digital capabilities, in the lower third of your TV screen you may be able to catch as many as four human images from an upcoming program. The lower third is now a promo-bar, where stations can deliver "coming up next" notes or remind viewers of a hit program that will air within the next few days. The lower third is also being developed as a place to signal audience members who are online, doing "enhanced viewing." *Wheel of Fortune,* the "hangman" game developed for TV by Merv Griffin, is using a piece of animation that will enable viewers to win prizes from their home computers during certain segments of the show. All we can say is, "OH, VANNA!"

When the messages are used as a written reminder, like "Fabulous Comedy Tuesday Nights," it may be annoying, but it's tolerable most of the time, unless one of these little reminders comes up in the middle of a particularly dramatic moment at the end of a program like *Law and Order: Criminal Intent.* And chances are, given this program's time slot, your younger household viewers will not be awake to notice.

But what has happened with the accelerated use of moving digital images is that occasionally you'll be watching a show, and suddenly an actor may give the audience a wave—from the cleavage of a character from whose ample bustline he has just emerged. Or out of a backpack. Or from under a car crash, like a digital leprechaun (or digi-zombie!). Worse, a **series** of little actors may begin walking into the frame, or appear and then walk off. The more movement (and tiny people), the greater the distraction for the viewer. If smiling cast members from another show are doing walk-ons on the bottom of the screen at the end of a critical scene in a drama, the efforts of the director and writers and the actors who are **supposed** to be there are damaged, if not altogether ruined. Or (ship)wrecked. Or, um, *LOST*.

Regrettably, the worst example is the otherwise entertaining mystery/crime show, *The Closer.* You see a tiny Kyra Sedgwick, in character as a police chief, walk onto the right-hand corner of the screen with a flashlight—which she then points right at the audience. You. The viewer may know it's a digital effect, but that doesn't stop that little fictional flashlight from making you feel as if a high-wattage, industrial one had just been shined in your face. Fortunately, the writing is so strong, and the plot twists so interesting, that the story will keep you hooked. It certainly won't be the promos.

So when anything happens in the "lower third" that has nothing to do with the program you and your family are watching, be sure to point this out to the other viewers in the room, get their feelings, and if the comment is something along the lines of "That drives me crazy!" don't just sit there. Jot down the date, the time, and the program and channel you were watching, and if you manage to recover from this distraction long enough to catch the ending of the show, make sure you watch the credits. That way, when you e-mail the network, you can at least ask that your comment be relayed to the producers of the show, and you'll have a name to include in your message.

Of course, you may have a hard time reading the credits, since many stations are minimizing the font so that they can promote the next show. Some networks are adopting credits-on-crawl. If your child were an actor or a writer on the show, and didn't get credit for his or her work, how would s/he feel? ASK.

ZAP

1. Count the number of moving items (spinning, walking, morphing, etc.) in the lower third of the screen between each commercial break (in other words, during the show itself.) If the "attack of the little people" makes your family want to throw large appliances at the screen, perhaps this is the time to draft that letter or e-mail to the network, station, or production company.

2. Let your kids explore those "Cool Brain Moves" mentioned earlier. For younger family members, try creating some images out of dots. There is an entire school of drawing (pointilism) based on this form of expression, and it's not as easy as it sounds. Some hints: If you use tiny dots, like the pointillists, your picture will be easier to see close up. But the bigger the dots, the farther away from the image you must be in order to "see" it.

3. Make a flip book, showing an animal (or whatever) in motion by changing the picture slightly in each frame. Make sure you make the flip book with sufficient pages to keep the "motion" sustained long enough to keep your Spongeheadz interested.

You can also go to the library or video/DVD rental outlet and find examples of early cartoons and stop-action animation. (Claymation and Gumbyesque oldies are fun, and your kids will be amazed that they actually **amused** kids "back in the day.") Then look at current cartoons (many of which are sent to Asia to be animated) and see how techniques have changed. Finally, jump to the present state-of-the-art works (now that you know how Pixar animation studios got its name!). There are excellent behind-the-scenes mini-documentaries on nearly every animated epic, such as the HBO special about *Finding Nemo*. A Google search of a movie title (*James and the Giant Peach*, *Toy Story*, and for older kids, Tim Burton's *The Nightmare Before Christmas*) can provide some resources.

We make TV commercials so people can go to the bathroom during our favorite shows...
Michael, grade 4

As we go to print, Pixar has just been acquired by Disney, in a move that truly deserves the title "(Animation) Monsters, Incorporated." You can go to Pixar's Web site and see excellent animated shorts, a trend that is likely to continue at both sites as the merger of the two giants moves forward. But the best way to appreciate the process of animation, either digital or old school, is to find a program that shows the work in process. (Watching Disney animators work with Robin Williams on *Aladdin* is as entertaining as the final outcome.) Check out *CARS* too. Then let your children create their own animation with some of the great software hitting the markets. (Boinx is a fave in the Seattle area.) There are Web sites where you can create a cartoon online and post it at a flash animation site.

The trip from doodle to digital is a great rainy-day ride.

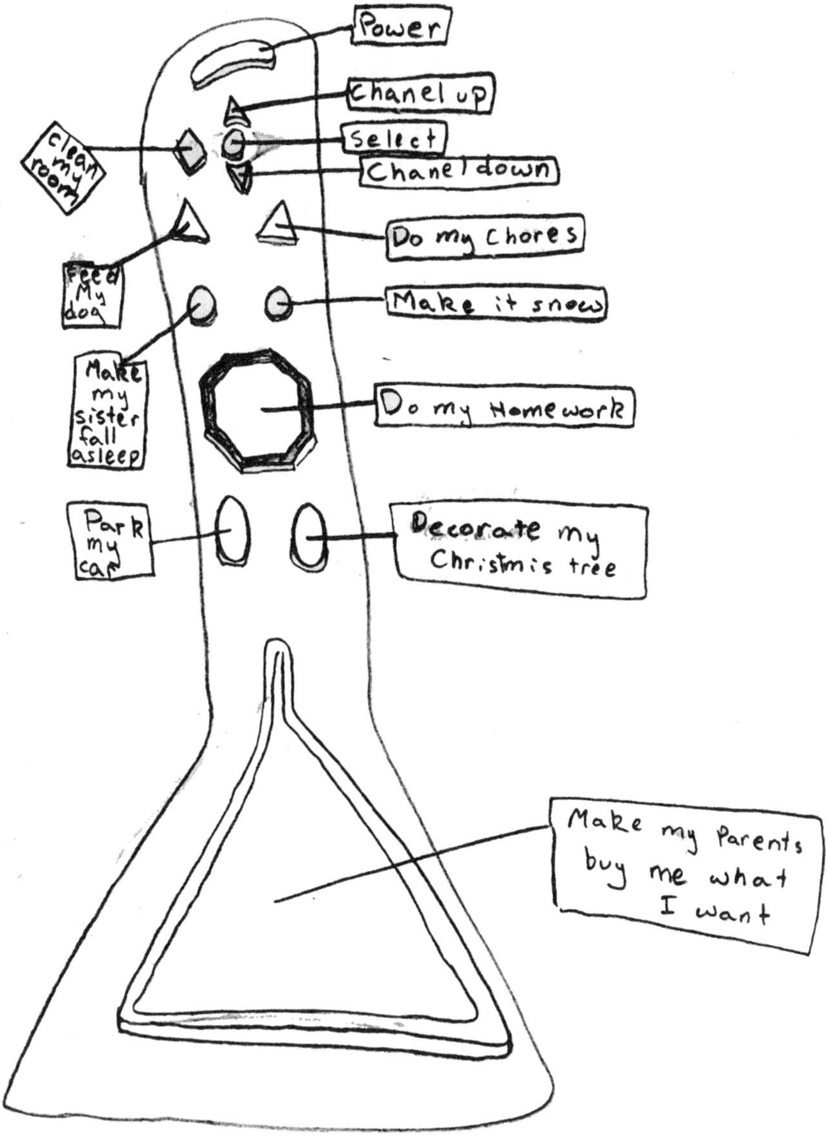

Power

Chanel up

Select

Chanel down

clean my room

Do my Chores

Feed My dog

Make it snow

Make my sister fall asleep

Do my Homework

Park my car

Decorate my Christmis tree

Make my Parents buy me what I want

Claire

POWER

"People have the power, people have the power!"

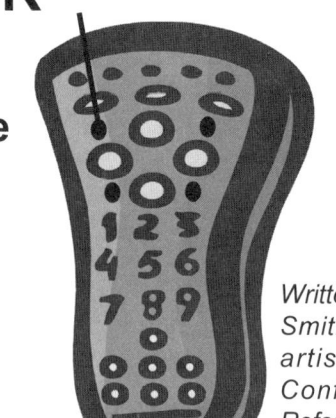

Written by rock legend Patti Smith, performed by the artist at the National Conference on Media Reform, May 2005, St. Louis

Most of us think of power in a variety of ways. The power bill is what pays for the electricity that runs the TV. But more than electricity is needed to put shows on the air, and there are layers of information that you can explore with children.

At one level, kids need to know that what puts a program on the air is a series of advertisers who want to reach a certain audience. Most kids (and adults) think that the show is "brought to you" by the advertisers.

No, **NO***, NO.*

In fact, it's the other way around.

Programming exists to bring an audience to the advertisers. (See the SELECT button.)

On a parallel level, kids need to know about the creative process, and that a show begins like everything else—as an idea that gets written down, discussed, and pitched to producers who put up the money to make it happen.

Parts are cast and a crew is hired to design and build sets and shoot the episodes. Behind the scenes are people who shop for clothes to dress the characters, electricians and tech people who make the mechanics of production happen, and public relations people to get the media to notice the launch of the new show. Go ahead: Try and count the number of people whose names roll at the end of any program and how many different departments and skill sets they represent.

On quite a different level are the companies that are buying the advertising minutes during the show—the sponsors. Sponsors wield a significant amount of power in getting a program to air and are important in keeping it there. This is why if there are objections to a show, consumers are likely to contact sponsors first. Angry viewers may announce to a station that they'll refuse to buy products from companies that sponsor the "offending" program. (However, in the author's opinion, letters are more effective.) And, if you know that a terrific show is about to be the victim of a well-orchestrated campaign, letters about the positive aspects of a show can save it from being shelved.

What surprises many people is how much power letters, e-mails, and phone calls from viewers have. While the projected numbers vary from station to station and network to network, each uses a similar formula to estimate actual viewer reaction. For example, let's say a television station receives five letters or e-mails about a particular show. The station in question may use a multiple of one hundred and consider that each letter represented one hundred people who felt the same way but couldn't be bothered to write. So advertisers react as if they are looking at five hundred unhappy audience members who may switch to another product until the show's problems are addressed. It definitely gets their attention.

But this process works both ways. There have also been excellent programs that were saved from the chopping block by massive letter-writing campaigns. This is another reminder to leave couch-potatohood behind—and to make certain the station, network, and advertisers hear your voice.

There is a governmental entity that is also supposed to listen to our voices. (Theoretically, all of them work for us, remember?) It's called the Federal Communications Commission, better known as the FCC.

Lynn Ziegler

If your kids think the FCC has ABSOLUTELY NOTHING to do with their lives (except for TV), tell them to guess again. FCC rules regulating radio, TV, wire, satellite, and cable include almost all electronic equipment that emits ANY kind of radio signal.

So, the FCC is involved when you

- Heat a breakfast waffle in the microwave

- Play with a remote-controlled airplane or car

- Pay tolls without having to stop at the booth (with a small plastic box attached to the windshield)

- Swipe a credit card at the gas pump

- Push a button in the car to open the garage door

- Lock your car with a remote entry system

- Print your kid's homework on the printer downstairs via a wireless home network

- Rent a video and have the clerk check to see if you have enough bonus points to get a free movie

- Pay the barista for that iced nonfat raspberry mocha using an electronic cash register and inventory control system

- Activate a home alarm system before going to bed

- AND WATCH TV

See? You have a lot of reasons to care about what the FCC does.

There is another reason we should be concerned about the FCC, and it's pretty wonky for a book for kids and families, but here goes: As we transition from analog to digital TV, the FCC will be auctioning off bandwidths, since digital "compression" of information makes it possible for more programming to get to your TV.

Why should you care? And who gets those bandwidths?

One reason these questions really matter is that even now, five years after 9/11, and a year beyond the Gulf Coast hurricane recovery fiascoes, first responders still cannot communicate with each other at disaster sites. Why? Their radios don't talk to each other. It's not a case of incompatibility; it's that there are no available bandwidths to turn over to first responders solely for emergency use. This is because we haven't done the changeover from analog to digital. Those analog bandwidths are needed, but the turnover date keeps getting pushed back—because of pressure from the broadcasters themselves. "Local broadcasting is a powerful lobby," says Norm Ornstein. "It's as if the broadcasters were given beachfront property by the Telecommunications Act." Currently, the changeover from analog to digital is scheduled for January 2009. But the "airwave auction" is expected to be completed before the end of 2006. Stay tuned. (See the "ZAP" section on page 29.)

Think of this as a process. Our children can learn about first responders **and** the First Amendment!

If media conglomerates are unwilling to quickly move forward into turning over the airwaves, and the same company that owns several stations in a market also publishes some newspapers, how do you get information that hasn't been filtered?

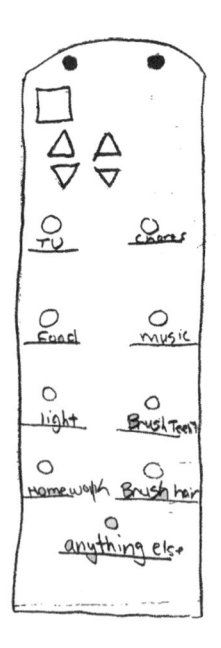

Alicia

Let's start with some definitions.

What are the Mass Media, and who owns them?

The mass media are communications systems that reach millions of people every day through sophisticated technologies like broadcasting, cable, and the Internet.

Broadcasting transmits radio and television signals of different frequencies over the public airwaves. Depending on the strength of the signal and the technology used, broadcasting encompasses everything from low-power community radio stations to satellite signals that are beamed anywhere in the world.

Cable transmits TV programming through fiber-optic cables. By the 1980s it had become the primary medium for television. Broadcast TV networks are now included as a basic part of cable service.

Film and video include both the photographic process for making movies and the videotape and "digital video disk" or DVD technologies. Today, films are viewed not only in movie theaters, but on television, via video or DVD players, and on computers (and soon, on cell phones).

The Internet is an interlocking system of computer networks that were originally connected by dial-up telephone lines. Today, cable companies offer high-speed Internet access (or "broadband") through their cables, and telephone companies offer high-speed DSL or "digital subscriber lines." The fight for "Internet neutrality" is now being waged in corridors of Congress—as those who want to keep the Net free and accessible take on the corporate giants looking to install toll booths on the digital highways.

Print media consists of newspapers, magazines, books, and, more recently, e-books. Despite the proliferation of electronic media, many people still like to read. (Say AMEN, somebody!)

The telecommunications issues facing our kids throughout their lifetimes and the rest of ours are going to center around teaching them to reclaim their airwaves. Activism needs to start early. **Like NOW**.

No chapter on POWER would be complete without a basic introduction to the FCC and media conglomeration, which many people feel lessens the number of viewpoints and voices heard since the FCC was created in 1934.

The FCC has five commissioners, appointed by the President—two from each party, with the chairman's position usually going to a commissioner from the party in power. As we go to print, the FCC has been challenged with rewriting a huge portion of the regulations that affect ownership (and thus diversity) of the airwaves.

When television first began in the United States, there were two broadcast networks—red and blue. They became CBS and NBC. NBC, which was, and is owned by General Electric (GE), split, and ABC was formed (which also ran third in ratings for some time.) But being in last place has a singular advantage: You are more willing to take risks and try a show that's "different."

Then came independent local channels. When cable arrived, numbers of stations expanded geometrically. When satellite dishes entered the scene, an even greater boomlet occurred. But there are many people who still believe that Bruce Springsteen had the situation nailed, when he sang "Five Hundred Channels, and Nothin' On."

Media conglomeration began its greatest growth in the 1990s. The following brief overview will offer a sampling of the six companies that control much of what we watch and hear.

AOL TIME WARNER

In January 2001, one of the largest mergers in corporate history made America On Line and Time Warner the world's biggest company. They own the entire Turner Entertainment Corporation, including four sports teams. They hold about 20 percent of the nation's cable television market. Those holdings include the Internet service provider America On Line, the Warner Brothers and New Line Cinema film production companies, and cable channels CNN, HBO, WB, Cinemax, Cartoon Network, TNT, TBS, and TCM. Among their fifty-two record labels are

Atlantic and Elektra; the twenty-four book brands include their own DC Comics, and magazines *Fortune, Sports Illustrated,* and *People.*

VIACOM

Viacom has been described as pitching "unbridled consumerism from cradle to grave." Harsh? Consider this: Viacom owns Nickelodeon, which is itself a brand that most kids can readily identify, and CBS, the network watched by most older Americans (with two hundred affiliates and global distribution.) In between are MTV, which reaches 342 million households worldwide, and VH1 (its chief "competitor"), BET, Showtime, and Comedy Central, home of *The Daily Show* and *The Colbert Report.* The twelve TV and film studios include Paramount, United Cinemas International, and Famous Players; a joint venture with Vivendi Universal with 104 cinemas in Europe, Japan, and South America; Blockbuster Video, with outlets in twenty-seven countries; two thousand book titles annually; 180 US radio stations, including Infinity: and Infinity Outdoor, the largest advertising company in the world. In January 2006, Viacom split into two companies: Viacom and CBS. Sumner Redstone is chairman of both companies.

In September 2006, there was new development. UPN and the WB, two independent channels with strong minority viewership, formed a new network: CW, for CBS and Time Warner. And yes, we all know why it isn't going to be called "the WC."

DISNEY

The Walt Disney Company would like to extend the Disney experience into almost every aspect of life. They have even built a town, Celebration, Florida—a $2.5 billion pre-planned village that will regulate everything from who can move in to how high your neighbor's hedges can grow. This takes the Disney brand and turns it into a lifestyle.

Disney's film companies include Disney, Touchstone, Miramax, Buena Vista, and four others. Their theme parks include Disneyland in California and Paris; Disney World Florida, MGM Studios, Disney's Animal

Kingdom (part of Disney World FL), World Sports Complex, twenty-seven hotels (with more than 37,000 rooms), two cruise ships, and the Disney Institute, where professionals can discover "the biz behind the magic." Disney owns ABC TV and Radio—ten TV stations and twent-nine radio stations. Disney Theatrical Productions include stage musicals *The Lion King* and *Beauty and the Beast*, as well as five magazine publishing groups and four newspapers. The Disney Channel broadcasts in eight countries, and it owns ESPN, which broadcasts to over 165 countries in Asia, Europe, and Latin America. Other channels include Walt Disney TV, Sportsvision Australia, and eight others, and the baseball team the Anaheim Angels. In summer 2006 Disney made a major (and expensive) acquisition: Pixar Studios (*Toy Story, Finding Nemo*).

BERTELSMANN

Their multimedia ad agency, Pixelpark, "brand manages" major clients, such as Adidas. Bertelsmann is the world's biggest publisher—it owns Random House, which ships a million books a day in the US alone, has book clubs across South America and Europe, and is a major publisher of science titles. It also owns the UK's Channel 5 and TV and radio stations across Europe, including the RTL Network (twenty-two TV stations and eighteen radio stations in ten countries.) Bertelsmann Broadband is exploring the convergence between TV and computers, and its Services Group includes consumer databases to call centers around the world. Subsidiary Gruner and Jahr publishes eighty magazines worldwide, from *Femme* to *Prima,* and owns nine newspapers across Germany and Eastern Europe. (A piece of their corporate history they would like to de-emphasize is that Bertelsmann was a sponsoring member of the SS and a major printer of Nazi material during the Third Reich.) Bertelsmann Music Group (BMG) operates in 54 countries; its US labels, in turn, own 200 labels worldwide. It owns the Web portal Lycos and worldwide online book shopping via **www.barnesandnoble.com**, and other ventures.

NEWS CORPORATION

"Our reach is unmatched around the world. We're reaching people from the moment they wake up until the time they fall asleep." (Rupert Murdoch)

News Corp owns FOX News and seven other news networks in the US. In the UK, it owns BskyB and Sky, with 150 channels and services; Australian channel FOXTEL; STAR TV satellite services, which reach 300 million people across Asia; Phoenix satellite TV; and four other channels that serve much of China. News Corp also broadcasts into India, Japan, Indonesia, New Zealand, Latin America, and Europe. FOX also owns DirecTV and cable channels National Geographic and Fox Movies. In addition to Harper Collins and seven other publishing houses, News Corp owns the following publications: *The New York Post* (US), *The Times, The SUN,* and *News of the World* (UK); one hundred national and regional titles in Australia, including *The Australian, The Daily Telegraph, The Sunday Tasmanian*, and sixty-seven suburban papers; The Independent Newspapers of New Zealand, as well as fifty-five national and community newspapers and titles, including those sold in Fiji and Papua, New Guinea. In entertainment holdings, FOX TV has twenty-two stations, and there are fourteen FOX entertainment companies globally, including Twentieth Century Fox. Finally, News Corp owns the Australian National Rugby League, the LA Dodgers, and numerous UK football clubs.

VIVENDI UNIVERSAL

Vivendi, better known as a giant in the privatized water industry (from Puerto Rico to Three Valleys Water in the UK) merged with media company Seagram in 2000. Vivendi Universal has taken "convergence" furthest—integrating film, music, and mobile phones. It also has big stakes in cable and wire companies that deliver these services. VivendiNet is the home of all the company's Internet projects, including **www.vizzavi.com** with Vodafone, combining the Internet, mobile phones, interactive TV **www.Education.com**, and music download site **www.MP3.com**. Universal Music Group has a 22 percent share of the global music market, in sixty-three countries, owning labels like Polygram, Geffen, A & M, Island, Decca, Deutsche Grammophon, MCA, and Motown. Havas, the publishing arm, owns sixty publishing houses, selling eighty million books and forty million CD ROMS per year. Vivendi Environment, the water and utilities group, also owns UK train service CONNEX and five "Universal Studio Experiences" from Barcelona to Beijing. Canal +, the leading French station, has fourteen million subscribers in eleven European nations. Universal Studios is global, owning theme channels like "Action and Suspense." Universal TV owns series like *Kojak, Miami Vice,* and *Columbo*; their theatres include the Cineplex Odeon chain and United Cinema International, as well as two major French mobile phone companies. Vivendi Telecom International has operations in Spain, Hungary, Monaco, Poland, and Egypt. Vivendi Universal has just joined forces with the DeVry Institutes to create new game programmers for the small (really small) screen entertainment companies. Vivendi also owns 26.8 million shares in TIME WARNER stock.

When this chapter was originally written, the estimated worth of each of these companies was in the tens of billions.

And *as you were reading this*, the estimated worth of *all* of these companies will have increased impressively. And folks—that's just the BIGGEST HALF DOZEN.

By this time, you and your SPONGEHEADZ must be numb—but not too numb to notice the crossover of TV, radio, newspapers, publishing, the Internet, and telecom businesses.

If the saying "All politics is local" resonates with you, consider this: In 2006, four companies control two-thirds of this country's news format radio programs. Two of these firms, Viacom and Disney, control major TV networks. Imagine this on a smaller scale, in your own home market. What does it mean when one company owns a newspaper, several radio stations, and a TV station? How likely is it that a "different" viewpoint will be heard?

And what happens when disaster strikes a local neighborhood? Here's a scary example.

In 2002, a train accident in Minot, North Dakota, spilled 210,000 gallons of hazardous material. When civil authorities called local radio stations to warn area residents about the toxic cloud, they found no one present who could make the announcement. Why? Clear Channel owned all six commercial radio stations in Minot, and none of its programming was local. In fact, the shows were being piped in from its national headquarters. In today's risky environment (natural disasters, chemical explosions, wildfires, hurricanes, floods), can you see how important this is? When local stations lose their

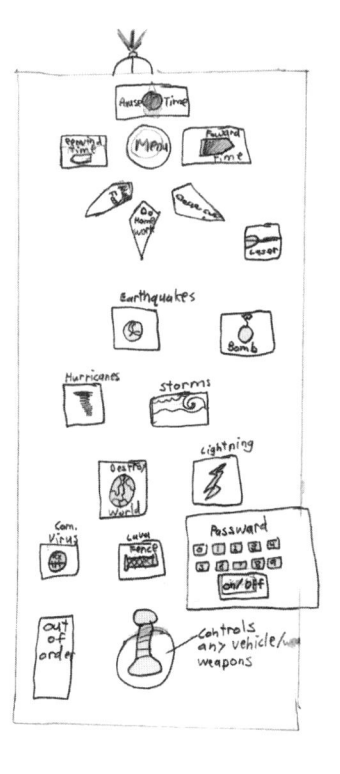

neighborhood connection, because they are simply acquisitions of an absentee landlord, the people lose. Big time.

This kind of thinking applies to the Internet as well and is the reason so many groups are campaigning for "Net neutrality." In fact, a Seattle-based company is designing software that will test for equal access and equal speed in reaching cyber-destinations. If you haven't already done so, now would be a very good time to contact your senators and representatives urging them in the strongest terms possible to support "Net neutrality," which will keep the Internet free from the folks who want to establish toll booths along what used to be called "the Information SuperHighway."

The need for fair, full representation and regulation is the reason the FCC exists. As telecommunication law is updated and rewritten in the opening decade of the twenty-first century, there is perhaps no more important time in history to get to know the FCC and its role in your life.

As this book goes to print, the FCC's new Chair, Kevin Martin, seems to be in favor of public input and media education, more so than his predecessor—but that may not be the case. His strategy, according to an article by Paul Riismandel in *Media Geek*, may not be quite as it seems.

Martin's strategy appears to be designed to undercut the public's power on the issue. The deadline for public comment on the FCC's media ownership review was September 22, 2006. The problem is that the public hearings, which are places where people can learn about media ownership as well as expressing their opinions, DIDN'T HAPPEN BEFORE THEN. Public opinion will come only AFTER these critical decisions are made. This is a smart tactic.

Martin's predecessor, Michael Powell, seemed to shut out the public from the process. The result was millions of postcards being sent to the FCC forcing an opportunity for reconsideration of media ownership guidelines. Martin, on the other hand, gives the appearance of embracing public input—**but only after the fact.** This deprives the public—viewers like you—of the tools to better form their opinions until **AFTER THE COMMENT DEADLINE.**

You can contact the FCC at **www.fcc.gov.**

ZAP 1. Have your kids call your local first responders and tell them they want to help them get their first responder bandwidths when the spectrum is auctioned off. Make it a class project, a family project, an "electronic citizen" project. Get your senators and representatives involved. Encourage your children, by following your example to work to reclaim the airwaves that really DO save lives.

2. Make a list of things your family enjoys using, eating, or having in your home. Then see what company makes each item and what other companies they own. This is not just an exercise in advertising (we'll get to that later), because if you show children how many products from one particular conglomerate are part of their daily lives, they will begin a learning process that will take them (and you) to the next step: understanding, ultimately, the influence of corporations, especially in terms of national policies. Yes, it's a big leap and a long trail. But, as the ancient Buddhist saying goes, "The longest journey begins with a single step."

3. Write to the FCC and tell the commissioners how you feel about media consolidation in your town. First, you'll need to look into which companies own which media outlets. Don't forget to include radio and newspapers! And make a trip to your PBS station to see what you can do to assist in fundraising. Have your kids check out the FCC Kids Zone, which offers an interesting and informative set of media histories—including the one for TV.

Thanks to Marjorie Heins and Neema Trivedi of the Free Expression Policy Project at the Brennan Center for Justice for their help with this chapter. Their excellent media fact sheets are available at **www.fepproject.org**.

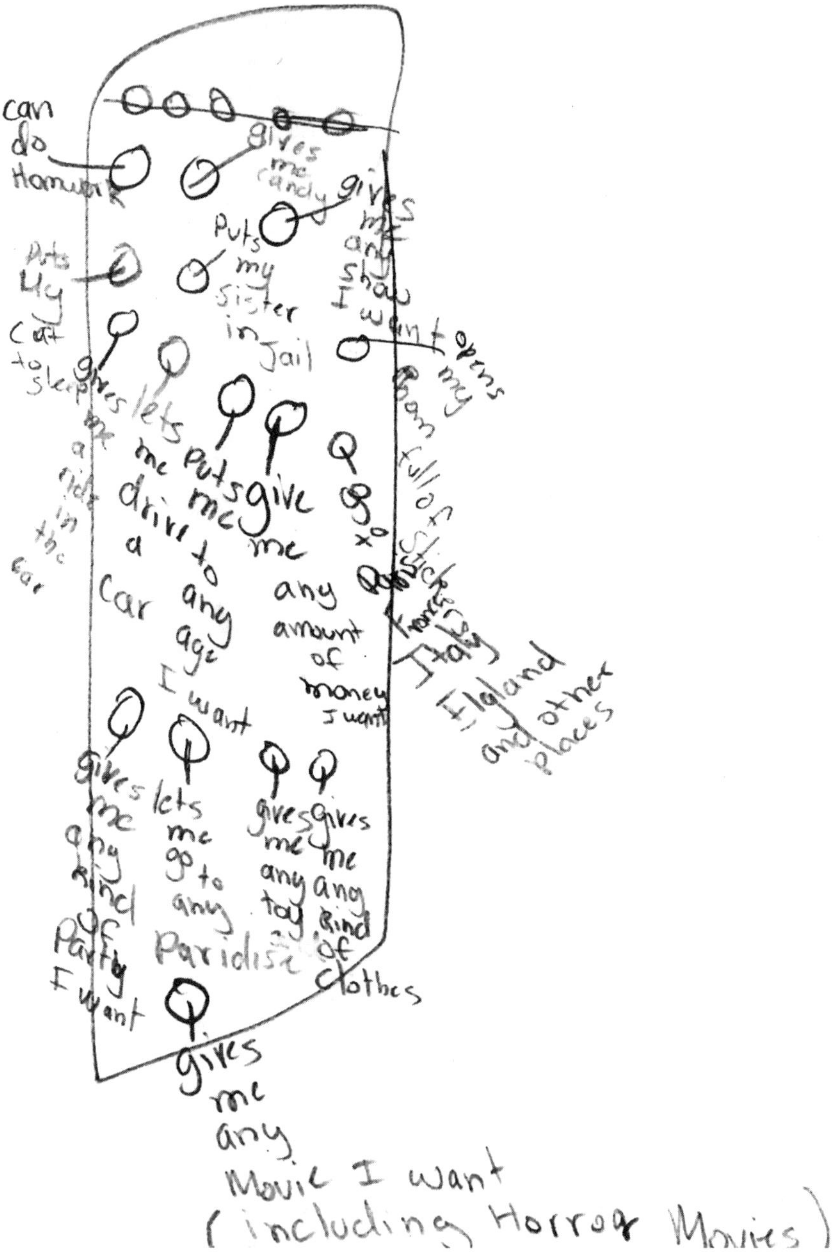
can do Homwork
gives me candy
gives me any show I want
Puts my sister in Jail
Puts My Cat to sleep
opens my room full of stickers
gives me a ride in the car
lets me drive a car
Puts me to any age I want
give me any amount of money I want
go to France Italy England and other places
gives me any kind of Party I want
lets me go to any Paridise
gives me any toy
gives me any kind of clothes
gives me any Movie I want (including Horror Movies)

Maggie

BALANCE

"Look, Daddy, they're doing it on purpose!"

Overheard by CNN Producer Rose Arce, as the second plane hit the WTC, September 11, 2001.

News is different now.

Twenty-five years ago, Ted Turner changed TV news forever with the introduction of a twenty-four hour news cycle. Instead of tuning in at noon, 5 p.m. and 6:30 p.m. (network news fills in the half-hour between local news casts), and 10 or 11 p.m., we can get the latest goings-on at any time of day or night. Not only that—all news outlets have Web sites that are refreshed up to the minute. (Some news sites actually read "Two minutes ago…") You can get updates via cell phones and pod-casts.

And you can read most newspapers online. This is fine, if you are a news junkie—and many adults are.

But if you're a kid…the news has become more disturbing than ever.

Adults break news down to three kinds: local, national, and global, although the last one is a relatively new consideration for many Americans.

But to kids, *all* news is local. In fact, news could happen down the street, and sometimes does. Unless you tell them that a reported disaster won't take place nearby because it is several states (or oceans) away, that's exactly what they may believe.

A case in point: During the first Gulf War, as world audiences watched bombs bursting over a city on the other side of the world, our children were really frightened. So Fred Rogers, (yes, *that* Mr. Rogers, in one of the smartest, most compassionate moves he ever made, and that's saying something!) made a special public service announcement. In it, he quietly explained to his target (pun intended) audience that there were no bombs falling in his—or any other American neighborhood. He quietly reaffirmed to children that here we were safe, and that no one would let anything bad happen to them. CNN, which had been airing the war live in our living rooms, aired Mr. Rogers' PSA and then cut back to the anchor desk—maybe a little too quickly. The male and female anchors were sitting there with their eyes glistening. Fred Rogers had told the anchors, the country, and the children exactly what we all needed to hear—that we were safe in our homes and our homeland.

Days later, ABC anchor Peter Jennings held a "Kids Talk About the War" question-and-answer session with kids of varied ethnic backgrounds. Jennings also made children's TV history when he arranged a "Kids Talk to the President" broadcast during the first months President Clinton was in office. The behind-the-scenes stories from that amazing program were as interesting as the event itself.

Jennings, who really believed in reaching out to children, had invited kids of nearly every faith and ethnicity to meet the new President, who had a twelve-year-old daughter of his own at the time. One of the invited girls, a Native American from an East-Coast tribe, had planned on asking him why car makers kept naming automobiles after Indian tribes (and she wasn't crazy about sports teams doing that, either). But when the moment came, she turned to the new President and asked him to recognize her nation, which had lost its federally recognized status, most likely due to declining enrollment. And for the first time in American history, a sitting President and a Native American child discussed tribal sovereignty, face to face, and had their conversation broadcast around the world. It was absolutely unforgettable TV.

Kids can learn to appreciate news. It is their window on their world, as well as ours.

Peggy Charren, the founder of Action for Children's Television, once told this author that *Nick News* was the only news show she'd ever seen "that could explain the Bosnian conflict so that everyone could understand it." Ditto the problems in the Middle East, say other fans of the show.

Linda Ellerbee has frequently been asked, "How is doing news for kids different?" With her Texan twinkle, she said, "News for kids is just like news for adults. Only better." In fact, Ellerbee's production company, Lucky Duck (for those who remember the rubber duck on her grown-up network newsdesk), has been creating the best news program for kids for more than a decade, bar none.

Peter Jennings, Fred Rogers, and Linda Ellerbee understood that children need to know what is going on in their world. Their work was, and is, at the forefront of an effort to help kids understand some of the forces that would shape their futures as adults. And they did it the

right way: by not avoiding the truth and by refusing to be condescending. They told it like they saw it and brought news for kids into
the twenty-first century.

Of course, TV news, along with a great many other parts of daily life,
changed after the events of 9/11. And children now understand that
horrible happenings **can** take place in their neighborhoods, whether
it is a natural disaster, an unspeakable multiple homicide, or a politi-
cally/religiously inspired explosion.

News is sometimes referred to as "the beast" (as in "the beast must
be fed"). The news animal is hungry 24/7. It feeds on events and
whatever the "flava" of the moment is. The problem with news, from
a business standpoint, is that it is not a profitable department. (Read:
NOT a money-maker to the bean counters who work for the company that owns the company that owns the company that owns the
station. This is a VERY abbreviated explanation of one of the many
problems of media consolidation.) So rather than meeting its original objective of providing good quality journalism, some TV news
morphs into infotainment.

Worse, in an effort to improve ratings (especially during sweeps), the
local news becomes a video buffet for other creative network projects
that may have nothing to do with your local community. Case in point:
No matter which network covers the Olympics, their network news
will have more "personal" athlete stories than the competition. In the
trickle-down to local news, that means more stories on area Olympic
hopefuls. This is not, in itself, a bad thing. But if the station is also
hyping a made-for-network TV movie on the challenges facing a particular (or fictitious) athlete, and airs it in prime time, and can sell
commercials at top dollar for that prime-time telecast, that promotional exercise keeps bean counters happy at all rungs of the corporate ladder. Obviously, the more money that can be made, the happier
they are. (To reiterate one of the opening lines of this book: **TV IS A
BUSINESS**.) But blurring the line between news and entertainment
becomes trickier by the hour in a culture that values celebrity more
than knowledge. This is not a good idea.

Perhaps the best way to explain news to our kids is like an old-
fashioned, woven pot-holder. You probably have an ancient one lying

around, the kind made of multi-colored loops. Check the drawer with bottle openers, cassette tapes, and other artifacts.

Take a good look. Lines overlap. For instance, environmental news may have a local focus, but there are environmental news stories that are national and global. And that makes them political, too. Political stories may have an impact on which schools get closed in your neighborhood—an education overlap. The under-funded libraries in those schools may be under pressure from local religious groups to offer (or not) books that preach "intelligent design" over evolution, so there is a religion/philosophy overlap. Some activists may be concerned about the availability (or lack thereof) of a chapter of the GSA (the Gay Straight Alliance). Others may have concerns about school health clinics that make birth control information and AIDS prevention material available— these are medical overlaps. That waffle-weave is infinite.

Children NOW, a media-savvy advocacy group, suggests ten tips about watching TV news with our kids:

Reality. News is the scariest thing on TV. Nicky, grade 6

1. Explore the age-appropriateness of the news you allow your children to see.

    Pre-schoolers (under age six) are just as likely to be afraid of what they see on the news as they are of dragons or other fictional menaces. Kids between the ages of six and ten are the most vulnerable news audience—they know the difference between fantasy and reality, but lack perspective. They may not worry about monsters under the bed any more, but they will (and do) worry about the monster who recently kidnapped a neighborhood child, as well as natural disasters and car accidents. Also, most children do not understand "frequency"— if they hear about break-ins, shootings, homicides, and other crimes in their area, (even if you are in a metropolitan area with millions of people), they will believe that these are common or frequent events. The world, then, becomes much scarier than it needs to be. Or really is. In fact, if one crime story is repeated five times in an evening—that can be five different crimes to a child.

SPONGEHEADZ: U & MEdia

Adolescents—tweens and teens age eleven and up—have become a great deal more knowledgeable about media, but disinformation from their peers (not to mention pressure) can lead to a considerable amount of confusion. They may think they want to understand the world in black and white, but the grey tones in between, particularly as they develop their own beliefs, can become pretty fluid. AND THAT'S OKAY, as long as we check in with our kids and ask them what they are experiencing, how they feel, and why. ALWAYS ask what made them look at a story from their particular angle. Your kids need more than peer validation—they need accurate info.

2. Watch or read the news with your kids. This lets you have some hands-on (not remote) control over how much they are exposed to!

3. Create an open dialogue. The best way to make sure kids know they are safe is to talk with them about what they see and hear. Don't make the discussion formal—make it a "chat opportunity" about things in their everyday lives. For instance, discussing a classmate with a progressive disease could launch a discussion about stem cell research. It really can be that simple.

4. Share your feelings about the news you see. If you start a conversation with "That news report about gun violence bothers me, because I don't think guns belong anywhere near kids," you may find out more about your child's thoughts and feelings.

5. Let your kids know the difference between news and reality. School violence gets lots of coverage, but there is only a one in two million chance that a child will be injured in a violent outbreak at school. Kids need to know that just because they saw it on the news doesn't mean it is going to happen to them.

6. Acknowledge your child's fears. And remind your child that you are there to keep him or her safe, along with teachers, neighbors, and first responders, like firefighters.

7. Explore the facts with your child. Need more details? GOOGLE!

8. Acknowledge the complexity of the news. Even the most informed parent will find it difficult to explain war, famine, and why politicians don't always tell the (whole) truth. But the more

people communicate, the better they understand. That goes for kids, too.

9. Select kid-friendly news sources for your child. "All news is not created equal" is a good slogan to remember. Local news may focus on crime and car crashes; network news may cover policy changes and global disasters. Again, in this author's opinion, *Nick News* on Nickelodeon is the best news show for kids.

    And there are lots of Web sites where kids can get news that is of high interest to them. Find them!

10. Balance your child's news diet. How does your child get news? Listening to the radio in the car on his way to school? Or seeing crime scenes on the news program that follows her favorite afternoon show? Season his or her news diet with perspective and communication—and a large helping of common sense.

In fact, here is where you can explore new ways to think about news.

"The TV network created by the people who watch it" is how Current TV bills itself and it is exactly that—short news pieces sent in to the Current TV studios. The young adults who host the "news pods," or segments, call it "VC2": V-C-Squared, for Viewer Created Content. Find out more about it at their Web site: **www.current.tv**. Current TV was started by former Vice President Al Gore and features some of the most interesting sites and sounds on and in the news world— incredible visuals, cheerfully casual interviews, and thought-provoking topics are just three of the many reasons to tune in. You can find more alternative news sites on Google, and you can also locate a list put together by this author on the ACME (Action Coalition for Media Education) Web site at **www.acmecoalition.org**.

Along these VC2 lines, CNN is launching "I-Report"—a policy that will simplify the process of getting a breaking story from your hand to the network (and the rest of the planet). By turning over images to CNN for broadcast use, the aspiring newsperson will be able to say, "I-Report—for CNN." (This project is sponsored by Dell in an effort to get people to engage with the company's newest products.)

This is the direction media is headed. More people have access to digital recorders of all kinds (camera phones, digital cameras, cameras on our computers) than ever before—we have media literally at our fingertips. Viewer-created content is no longer accidental, like when a police car-mounted camera catches an unexpected incident or excessive force, or a security camera records an abduction. More and more people are beginning to understand that recording history and making news can be just a click away, and that finding, shooting, and posting a story is a headline in the hand.

Kids can find and make news, too. Encourage them to do so. CNN's morning anchor, Daryn Kagan, is leaving CNN to start a news Web site that focuses on positive news. The site, **www.darynkagan.com**, will launch in November 2006.

OTHER NEWS ISSUES:

WAR: We are going to be in Iraq and other parts of the Middle East for a long time, whether it is in a "war" capacity or not. Your children will eventually know a victim of critical injury (or worse) of one of our current conflicts. How you handle this topic will depend on the age of your child and the cost of war s/he eventually must confront. But never forget, as a voting parent, that you can make informed decisions only when you have accurate information, and your children deserve to know what you think about *any* armed conflict—and why.

VNRs: Video News Releases (VNRs) are placed into the news cycle by corporations and governmental entities, and they frequently look like news reports. **They aren't.** Although these items are supposed to carry an attribution as to the supplier of the information, this protocol is not always followed.

You might ask why it's a bad thing for government to pay for VNRs, articles by columnists, and other propaganda techniques without complete and proper disclosure to the viewer/listener/reader. According to Susan Rogers, editor/publisher of **www.medialiteracy.com**, it's simple to explain:

"Because it's government covering itself, that's why," says Rogers, quoting a phrase from an article in the *Sacramento Bee* and added, "It struck me as a great way to immediately convey the difference between an actual reporter covering something, OR NOT. It really conveys the hidden agenda concept concisely and quickly."

"You think you are getting a news story, but what you are getting is a paid announcement," said Susan A. Poling, managing associate general counsel at the GAO (the U.S. Government Accountability Office). "What is objectionable about these is that the viewer has no idea that their tax dollars are being used to write and produce this video segment."

Wondering if you've seen VNRs? Sure you have! Their producers include the Department of Health and Human Services (the Medicare Drug campaign), and the Drug Control Office, whose anti-drug campaigns even included a live intro to be read by the local station anchor. Some local TV stations facing staff cutbacks sometimes aired the slickly produced packages without a single word to indicate that the "reporter" giving out the information did not work for the station, but was, in fact, an independent government contractor (who was, perhaps, looking to break into the real "news biz").

ALWAYS QUESTION THE SOURCE. As this book goes to press, the FCC is about to open hearings on "fake news." The best resource (so far) is available for download at: **www.prwatch.org**. It's called *Fake TV News: Widespread and Undisclosed. A multimedia report on television newsrooms' use of material provided by PR firms on behalf of paying clients,* by Diane Farsetta and Daniel Price, for the Center for Media and Democracy. Many people are not aware of the cozy relationships between pharmaceutical companies and some members of the medical community, the influence of the tobacco and alcohol industries on ad-buying decision-makers (think SuperBowl and NASCAR), and chemical companies masquerading as "green" industries. How green your lawn is takes second place to how green the company's bottom line is. Commercials constructed to mimic breaking news— presented from a fake anchor desk or news set, especially regarding health and safety products—are ***BOGUS.***

ENVIRONMENTAL NEWS: Our children will be dealing with the consequences of global climate change for the rest of our lifetimes, their lifetimes, and their children's lifetimes. The situation has become so serious that global warming and changes in the ocean levels are a forecast now, not a myth. You should find it disturbing that, as recently as 2005, NASA scientists who had been pointing out the visible damage to the polar ice caps had their work "edited" or "revised" and saw sections of their work deleted—because the scientists disagreed with the Bush administration's assertion that global warming hadn't been "proven" yet.

> **The first line of NASA's mission is to understand and protect the planet.**
> Jim Hansen, Scientist, NASA, on why he ignored the Bush administration's efforts to restrict his comments on evidence of accelerated climate change

In 2006, this situation is changing, and global warming discussions are quickly becoming "climate crisis" talks. With the release of the fictitious *The Day After Tomorrow* in 2005 and the documentary *An Inconvenient Truth* in 2006, the tide of opinion is turning. There is a sea-change in the American perspective, more in line and on line with the rest of the people on the planet. It's about time. (See the button marked "CLEAR.")

> **We've raised a generation that has learned to absorb information at a speed that was heretofore unthinkable.**
> Rob Cohen, Film Director

PROPAGANDA: Propaganda is defined in *Wikipedia* as "a specific type of message representation, directly aimed at influencing opinions, rather than impartally providing information." Originally the term was a neutral one, describing the spread of information that supports a certain cause. Over time, however, the term morphed into a more negative interpretation—the dissemination of false or misleading information in favor of a particular cause.

Strictly speaking, a message does not have to be untrue to qualify as propaganda. *But it may leave out so much of the truth that the statement becomes highly misleading*. This is known as a "sin of omission"—you only get the part of the truth that supports the speaker's viewpoint, and the rest is left out.

Individually, propaganda functions as self-deception, like a padded résumé or an exaggerated, overblown story, featuring the storyteller as a superhero. Culturally, propaganda can be released into the public conversation by misleading statements from politicians, pundits, business leaders, and/or religious leaders. Propaganda can fuel radio talk shows, debates, punditry…and can lead to erroneous policy decisions by government and other groups of well-intentioned yet misinformed people who got only part of the story. Knowing the difference between "news" and "propaganda" is critical during a time of great conflict. Many people will be disappointed to know that millions of tax dollars were used by the U.S. government to plant positive stories in mainstream newspapers about the Iraqi conflict. A firm (named after a beloved U.S. President) was hired for just this purpose.

Surprised? You shouldn't be. A well-known minority columnist was paid $250,000 to discuss only the good points of the No Child Left Behind Act just before it was signed into law. His syndicated columns were dropped from national papers once this unethical practice was exposed.

That is not how a "free press" is supposed to work.

Political ads are another kind of propaganda, and, as we enter the media-driven election cycles of the new century, we need to assess what we see and hear and then ask…**WHAT'S MISSING?**

News becomes even more vital to democracy in an election cycle.

The election that took place in 2000 was unlike any other in American history. The story about it began with a phone call on Election Night. Comedy Central had jokingly called it "Indecision 2000." And then life started imitating art.

It was a FOX News employee (and relative of the Republican presidential candidate) in Florida who first reported that Florida's electoral votes had made it a "red" state.

Other stations, not wanting to be scooped, jumped on that bandwagon, not knowing that there were more than a hundred thousand Florida voters who had been disenfranchised. This led to the longest "undecided" election in United States history, and the unique result of having one candidate installed by a Supreme Court decision by five justices—some of whom had been nominated to the nation's highest court by the candidate's father—a former President himself.

In the years since 2000, the efforts to help the electoral process go through a technological evolution are anything but comforting. Your children probably already are as technically adept as you are, and they will leave you in digital dust as news becomes portable on cell phones, PDAs, and MP3 players.

So they also need to remember that when one company has close ties to a political party and is responsible for voting machines that can be hacked and manipulated, questions about voter verification need to be raised and answered. Since 2000, efforts at election reform have hiccupped and stalled. There are still no laws mandating a paper trail to avoid legendary issues like "the hanging chad" or the "butterfly ballot," which will someday be obscure pop-ups in a history DVD or a trivia question on *Jeopardy*. A digital footnote—except for the people who lived through it.

Children understand accuracy. And they have a vivid, innate sense of fairness. As adults, we may find it difficult to live up to their high standards, but we owe it to them to try. They understand, at some level, that as much as they would like to, Mom and/or Dad cannot manage

miracles. But with some creativity, energy, and positive thinking, families can manage to promote the idea of an informed democracy, where everybody's vote **really counts**.

Otherwise, a line by some aging British rockers, "Here's the new boss. Same as the old boss," makes their song title a cautionary tale**: Don't Get Fooled Again.**

PAUSE

 1. This experiment was done in a real newsroom, by no less a legend than the *Washington Post*'s former executive editor Ben Bradley (of Watergate story fame). He asked the staff to go through the newspaper and mark all the stories one of three ways with what we now call "emoticons." Positive stories got a "happy" face; negative, or worrisome stories got a "sad" face; and neutral (neither good nor bad news) got a face with a straight line for its mouth. Then they went back through the paper, and counted up the number in each category.

Surprise! There was more positive than negative news, then, as now. You wouldn't know it to watch TV!

This is the kind of activity that can be done at all ages and reading levels. First, try it with your local newspaper. That's a good starter-demo for our kids that the world is not quite as frightening a place as the twenty-two minutes of local or network news would have them believe.

This can be done even more readily with TV news programming. Just divide the newscast into four segments: local news, national and world news, sports, and weather. Many news shows still end with a "kicker," an amusing story at the end (frequently unusual animal stories get saved for this). Then ask your family a simple question: "Is there more good news than bad? Why or why not?" As they say in the news biz, "The answers may surprise you."

2. Kids can also do their own newscasts on what's important to them. Ask them to divide the day into school, home, activities (sports, music, whatever), and weather. Ask them for the part of the day that made them laugh as the kicker. If you have video gear of any kind (camera or phone), record one of these, save it, and send it to grandparents, family, and friends. It will be a time capsule on your family life that you can enjoy years from now.

And GO LOCAL! Visit your community cable access channel, ask for a tour, and find out how you can sign up for production courses. Once you do, you may be able to have your child's work appear on your local community access

station. Renting the equipment from a community access station is a fraction of what it costs through a commercial outlet, and the experience of creating programming is well worth the effort.

In fact, one of the production books offers this bit of great news:

Every week, thousands of community groups and over one million individuals produce more than twenty thousand hours of new local programming for cable access stations nation-wide. That's more than all programming produced by ABC, NBC, CBS, FOX, and PBS COMBINED. Get out there! (Thanks to ACME member Rob Franzoni for this info.)

3. Explore new places where video is posted, such as YouTube, (recently purchased by Google!) at **www.youtube.com**, and **www.flickr.com**. The May 2006 *WIRED* magazine had an outstanding list published this spring (with Al Gore on the cover) that will keep you experimenting and exploring 24/7. Here are some examples:

Newgrounds (**www.newgrounds.com**) - Great collections of flash animation

ifilm (**www.ifilm.com**) - One of the original video clip sites

MobiTV - For $10 a month, MobiTV will stream thirty channels to your cell phone. (It's like carrying a tiny TV in your pocket.)

These sites are increasing daily. Check them out!

Looking for a way to put the news in perspective? And to bal-ance it with an acknowledgement that good things happen? Check out "This Week In History" at **www.peacebuttons.org** The site is a collection of events to demonstrate that "we are part of a rich heritage" of "advocating peace and social justice." The site includes large and dramatic events (Nelson Mandela's freedom from prison, for example) as well as lesser known ones, like the anniversary of the end of the grape boycott by United Farm Workers, and the signing of the Americans With Disabilities Act. The free weekly news-letter guarantees you'll have positive developments in social issues to share with your kids.

Toys

candy

M&M

Skittles

Makes my Brother dissaper

Make my sister disaper

Ice cream

Laptop

Butter finger

Fast Food

DO choures

NN

DO My Homework

Game

Gives me what ever I want

NP

Watch what ever I want

Groom MY cat

Neo-Pets

clean MY ROOM

Computer

What-ever

Amanda

COLOR

"Please don't believe the hype. Everything in this world ain't black and white.

Everybody ain't a stereotype Just because I look wrong I'm about to do right..."

Ice Cube
Theme song from FX's
Black.White.

"It's *wrong* to say *any group of anything* is all the same." - Teacher of the Year and outstanding jazz musician Fernando P., schooling cast member Bruno on his simplistic generalizations. *Black. White.*

TV started out in black and white. Even in its most primitive form, TV was able to show that, in America, there were white people **and** people of color. But TV couldn't quite be called "diverse" and certainly didn't earn that description.

When television began, almost everyone on the TV screen was white, and that didn't change for a surprisingly long time.

Amos & Andy, an early "black" program, was dissed by its critics even before it morphed from a radio show to TV. In 1953, those critics, among them the NAACP, felt that the weekly episodes were hardly more than a pixilated minstrel show. Yet, according to an excellent documentary, *TV in Black: Parts 1 & 2,* the show, however flawed, provided opportunities for black actors to be seen and heard. Further, the show featured characters who portrayed black lawyers, judges, entrepreneurs, and successful professionals. However, when the show left the air, it took years for black actors to be cast in similarly representative roles.

In the rest of the television's "larger picture" (which, back then, was very small!), black people were excluded from character lists and story lines, and they were excluded from writing the shows as well. So, you had teams of white, male writers putting words and gestures on paper for the few black actors the networks hired. But the excitement of seeing people of color on TV was still celebrated in African-American communities. The documentary describes families rushing into the living room to catch a black actor or performer—ANY black actor or performer, even in stereotypical roles—with pride.

Other races weren't represented on a regular basis at all, and *if* they appeared on camera, they were in service roles. That includes Tonto, the stereotypical, monosyllabic, anything-but-equal Native American companion of the Lone Ranger.

But TV was about to become the teacher some of us have always believed it could be. In 1956, a quiet woman named Rosa Parks, who had prepared for her moment in history by attending workshops on civil disobedience, refused to move from her seat on a city bus, as local law demanded. She was a visible, living example of human dignity and performed her act of civil disobedience at great personal peril. Her stand—ironically, to remain seated—led to the Montgomery, Alabama, bus boycott, and black workers walked to their jobs for more than a year to protest the segregated transportation system. In the forefront of the civil rights movement was a brilliant young minister, the Reverend Martin Luther King, Jr., and his activist wife, Coretta Scott King, who spoke in Rosa Parks' behalf.

As civil rights legislation and voter registration became national concerns, television played an increasingly important role. Many people believe that, during the protests against African-American voter registration, it was the images of white southern police turning fire hoses and dogs on peaceful protesters that woke up America to a sea-change that needed to happen.

The intent of this book is not to explain the turmoil of the 1960s to your children. They already know about Dr. King. Rosa Parks and Coretta Scott King, two of the author's role models, both died as this book was being finished, and the work of this trio of heroes is celebrated and honored in every page.

TV played a part in these tumultuous times. You can explain to your children that if Americans had not seen images of prejudice and racism for themselves, as they happened, civil rights for people of color would have taken longer to become law. And, obviously, the struggle isn't over.

TV's ability to expose injustice didn't end with the passage of the Civil Rights Voting Act of 1965. The Voting Rights Act (VRA) came up for renewal in 2006, and was renewed, but only after last-minute efforts by some Southern conservatives to block its passage. Keep in mind that this was mere months after a major, predominantly African-American city was nearly eradicated in this nation's worst natural disaster. Hurricane Katrina hammered the Gulf Coast, but it was the failure of New Orleans' levees that killed more than a thousand people, and forced the relocation of hundreds of thousands of Gulf Coast residents.

The people who did not have the means to leave the city before the storm hit were overwhelmingly people of color. So were the people who spent hellish days and nights in the SuperDome, as were many of the people whose unidentified remains languished in make-

> **How present the past is, in the present.**
> Anderson Cooper,
> *CNN 360*

shift morgues in the Gulf Coast area. Some of the neighborhoods hardest hit, and least likely to be rebuilt, were the former communities of people of color.

One of the most powerful records of this disaster can be found in Spike Lee's documentary for HBO: *When The Levees Broke: A Requiem in Four Acts.* Parents should consider pre-screening it before sharing it with younger family members: the footage is heartbreakingly graphic, as is the language, but it must be seen to understand what really happened to a major American city in a new century (and on this administration's watch.) The DVD is available through HBO, and needs to be considered as living history—and an inspiration to "never forget." Some groups are asking that, until all the victims of this disaster are compensated, counseled and economically stabilized, we can *all* wear Mardi Gras beads, all year round, in solidarity with the people of NOLA. It's hopeful, joyous and eye-catching—and it's catching on.

And when the rescue efforts finally got under way (way too little, way too late) the faces the country saw on the news were predominantly people of color, stranded on rooftops, in stadiums…in crisis. Television news has more than proved its worth in documenting disasters like this one on the home front and around the globe. The coverage took in more than the disaster—it exposed levels of poverty in twenty-first century America that many people didn't believe existed.

(Want more info? Visit the Web site: **www.colorofchange.org**.)

But as amazing, horrifying, and moving as Katrina coverage became, there were moments of "cosmic instruction" that many people saw, but most people missed.

For example, two pictures were broadcast showing people wading through the water with foodstuffs in bags. In one picture a black man was seen dragging a plastic bag through the water. He was described as a "looter." The second picture showed a white young man and woman with similar plastic bags being dragged through the water. They were described as "people who had gone out to find supplies."

Nearly every media literacy expert in this country (including this one) as well as news anchor Anderson Cooper and comedians Carlos Mencia and Dave Chappelle cried, "FOUL!" The fact that this particular scenario received the coverage that it did reflects well on the public's clear need for media literacy, since this kind of racism occurs too frequently and needs to be brought to the attention of any station on which it appears.

Returning to our historical overview of TV, we can see that eventually, some of the racial landscape of TV began to change. Too slowly, of course, but even the most incremental progress was noted. A young, black male actor became the first sidekick to a white leading actor: *I Spy* brought Bill Cosby to television, and the concept of a main character as a person of color began to take hold. Diahann Carroll became *Julia*, a widowed black nurse left to raise her children on her own. Then along came Norman Lear, who created a bigot named "Archie Bunker," played by Carroll O'Connor, who said out loud the biased remarks people said in private conversation. He exposed the prejudices of white America every week and managed to be shown the error of his ways, in every episode, with humor. His stubborn ignorance played out in vivid contrast to his long-haired, liberal son-in-law, "Meathead," played by Rob Reiner, another actor about to enter politics. Each week, the turbulence of the times played out against the backdrop of this struggling New York family—the women's movement, the anti-war movement, the culture wars painted in psychedelic colors, including the rainbow cast members. *All in the Family* gave Archie Bunker African-American neighbors—who thrived, and eventually "moved on up to the East side." *The Jeffersons* were so popular that they became a successful spin-off and gave audiences an opportunity to hang out with an "upwardly mobile" black family. But a patronizing undercurrent was still evident in other shows.

The show that launched the career of recent gubernatorial candidate Gary Coleman, *Diff'rent Strokes*, featured a wealthy white Manhattan doctor who adopted two black kids. No wonder African-Americans and other minorities were worried about their children losing their connection to their heritage! TV still filtered culture through a white lens.

Remember, TV was born less than a century after the Civil War. It was a long time before audiences finally resonated with the fact that, while European immigrants had come to the United States voluntarily, African Americans had made a different kind of crossing. Poverty, indentured servitude, and ethnic prejudices were harsh for all immigrant communities. But slavery was another thing altogether. And it still has cultural echoes today.

Fortunately, in 1967, TV served up a program to help young audiences consider a rainbow of skin colors. Its name was ***Sesame Street.***

It may be difficult to believe, but when *Sesame Street* first appeared nearly four decades ago, there were parents who wouldn't let children watch it because, as one person told me, "There are so many blacks." Thankfully, those people were about to see the real magic of *Sesame Street* go to work: the characters, like people everywhere, came in all different colors. Not just brown, black, yellow, red, and white, but blue and green and fuschia and purple. What happened? Kids noticed how cool the differences were, and then got down to the business of getting to know (and love) each one.

Sesame Street not only had characters of all colors and ethnicities, it had CREATURES of all tints and types. It had friendly people, animals, and monsters and was brought to its audience not by sponsors, but by, for example, the letters Z and L and the number 4. The cast was culturally diverse, with men and women, old and young characters, and a stellar list of guest appearances by A-list talent that reads like *Who's Who in Entertainment*. You haven't really appreciated the alphabet until you watch Patti LaBelle croon, "Oh, How I Miss My X."

Years later, an animated Nickelodeon series called *Doug* took the *Sesame Street* rainbow philosophy to its next step, and every animated cast member was a different color—neon green, chartreuse, strawberry, purple. And ORANGE you glad? Kids GOT IT. No matter what color you were on the outside, what really mattered was who you were on the inside.

This is not to discourage **in the least** a sense of pride in ethnicity, culture, or heritage. Our children are growing up in a multi-racial, multicultural global community that becomes smaller every day. The people who were teenagers in the mid-sixties are now baby boomers in their mid-fifties, and hardly any of them could have predicted that their children or grandchildren could walk into their bedrooms and play a game online, in real time, with a kid on another continent.

The screen does not ask the color or culture of the user. But access to technology is as uneven as education itself, and much more work needs to be done in providing all kids and families quality environments for **both**.

The days when people could say, "Of course I've seen people of color/ethnicity. I've seen them on TV!" are winding down. But as hard as this may be to believe, there are people in this country who have never met ten people of different racial heritages *in their lifetimes*. (But they've "seen them" on TV. Sometimes they are people of color being arrested on FOX's *COPS*, or on the news, being herded out of a truck or a cargo container for making an illegal entry to the U.S.)

Well, seeing "them" on TV is not enough. It's not the same thing as knowing people, visiting them at home, going to the store together, or spending a day in their company. It's only by celebrating our differences AND our common ground that we genuinely connect.

In January of 2006, Dr. Phil McGraw talked to a man who was horrified that his daughter was about to have a biracial child. But after being invited into the home, the church, and the life of the "other" soon-to-be grandparents, the man was not only able to accept his daughter's choice, but went absolutely bonkers about his gorgeous grandchild once she arrived.

In 2006, a new TV program called *Black. White.* began a six-week run. Through some terrific makeup, cosmetic enhancements, and language coaching, two families exchanged races, living under the same roof as they ventured out as members of each other's cultural/genetic communities. It was a remarkable journey, not only for what was learned—but what wasn't. Look for it on DVD and watch it with your family.

And the creator of the film *Super Size Me* has a show called *Thirty Days*, in which people experience different lifestyles for a month. When a homophobe goes to live in a gay community in San Francisco, when a devout Christian travels (through an airport, no less) in traditional Muslim garb to live with a Middle Eastern family, when an urban, SUV-owning energy consumer lives on an organic farm without artificial, chemically developed items like makeup, toothpaste, and deodorant, with only solar power to run anything electric—**some kind of learning takes place**. The 2006 season will feature an Immigration and Naturalization Service (INS) agent who suddenly ends up living with a family of undocumented workers (he refers to them as "illegals"). If there is a better way to promote human understanding and experience than by slipping into each other's skin, or moccasins, as the old saying goes, TV will eventually show it to us. For now, experiencing someone else's life is a very promising beginning.

CHILDREN LOOK FOR FACES *LIKE THEIR OWN*. If they don't see their own ethnic group represented, they identify with another minority character. As was pointed out in the beginning of this chapter, TV may have started out in black and white, but there are other colors as well.

It is only in the past decade or so that Asian-Americans have been able to see a lessening of stereotypical portrayals, such as Chinese laundries and "ninja" anything. If you talk to Asian high school students, you'll find that one of the stereotypes they are uncomfortable with now, much to the dismay of their parents, is "straight-A geek."

As the Latin population increases in number and influence, there is more connectivity among youth, and that is reflected not only in programming, but in news coverage. As this book was being finished, Latino students took to the streets to protest proposed changes in immigration laws that many families felt labeled them as lawbreakers. One young Latina was seen holding up a sign that read, "I am an immigrant—NOT A CRIMINAL."

> Do you see faces like your own on TV?
> I did. Amanda, grade 6
> NO. Tyler, grade 6
> No, I have not seen my face. McKinzie, Grade 4
> Native faces? No. Aaron, grade 6

The expansion of cable and satellite offerings means that this nation's Spanish-speaking citizens can enjoy *Univision* and see additional programming in their own language. *Sesame Street* has been counting in Spanish for decades, and Nickelodeon's *Dora, The Explorer* began teaching Spanish phrases to preschoolers a decade ago. As more family programming written by actual members of the Spanish-speaking community is created, the better the viewer is

served. Brown actors are no longer limited to acting parts as drug pushers or gang leaders in the barrio or "Latin lovers." In fact, when *The West Wing* ended its successful run, the President was a newly sworn-in man whose last name was Santos. (Keep in mind that South Africa, with its horrific history of apartheid, elected a black man to its highest office soon after apartheid ended. But the first American presidential candidate of color was Congresswoman Shirley Chisolm, a fact that most American students rarely remember.)

Ellen Sirleaf-Johnson, who was recently elected the first woman President of Liberia, overheard the following conversation during one of her trips to the United States.

An American child, upon learning that Sirleaf-Johnson was not only a black woman, but President of her country, asked his mother (to the delight of Sirleaf-Johnson), "Mommy, when are we going to catch up with Africa?"

"In time," the wise mother replied. "In time."

Real politics must eventually echo the diversity of our changing country.

Vietnamese people can watch TV in Vietnamese; Japanese can see Japanese shows. There are Middle Eastern and Russian channels. Ditto Chinese, Korean, German, French, Italian, Argentine, Irani, African, and a host of other ethnic communities, including Indians, as in "citizens of India."

You can see every kind of ethnic group on TV—except for one.

Native Americans.

When *Northern Exposure* ended its run on the airwaves, it left a huge video vacuum for all of the Northern Hemisphere's indigenous peoples. (Canadians refer to tribes, respectfully, as *First Nations*. Most American tribes interact with the United States government on a nation-to-nation basis, as sovereign entities.) These are the people who were misnamed "Indians" by a white European who thought he'd made the passage to India.

SPONGEHEADZ: U & MEdia

On television, the stereotyping of Native Americans took place not only in live-action programs, but especially in cartoon form. Since cartoons are basically caricatures that move, physical and cultural stereotypes were exaggerated until the stereotype became more prominent than the character itself. Native Americans were depicted as hawk-nosed, feather- and loincloth-wearing, tomahawk-wielding, monosyllabic people, who were frequently left in any scene without much meaningful dialogue. There was a frequent implication, and more often an outright depiction, that "they" were lazy, violent, drunk, or all of the above.

When they appeared in Westerns on TV, the actors cast as "Indians" were Italian (or vaguely Mediterranean-looking) or Mexican—almost never genuine indigenous people. Not much effort went into research on different tribes, their customs, and their communities. "Indians" were easy to "package" for TV—a tipi, a horse, a loincloth and headdress—and really stupid (almost grunted) lines. The music was a dead giveaway—as soon as you heard a drummed

four beat (THUMP-thumpthumpthump THUMP-thumpthumpthump), you were in "Indian Country."

Most storylines about Native Americans covered only the European perspective, placing white women in danger of being "ravaged by savages," needing to be rescued by a white man in a uniform. None of what really happened after "First Contact" made it onto film (and then TV) until the last decades of the twentieth century.

There is not a monolithic "Indian." When you talk to your kids about First Nations, Native Americans, or indigenous peoples, always be certain to ask for the specific name of the tribe you're discussing. Understand that many tribes have sovereignty rights, which include the right to communicate on a nation-to-nation basis with local, state, and federal entities. If there is a Native American community near your town or city, see what part of their history, if any, is being seen through a twenty-first century lens.

Television has been making strides in celebrating diversity among our tribal nations. There have been excellent miniseries by Steven Spielberg and terrific documentaries by Native filmmakers. Feature films like Sherman Alexie's *Smoke Signals* are sometimes the first views of **contemporary** Native life that people have seen since the early days of TV.

Left to their own devices, kids can use TV to undo generations of stereotypes and misunderstandings. The following is a true story.

Eight weeks after 9/11, a plane crashed on Long Island. The community had already lost a hundred firefighters and first responders—in fact, the funerals were slowing down, and the holidays were coming fast, holidays that would mark the first of the rest of the lives of survivors and grieving families. And here was a smoking piece of wreckage, very visibly a plane, that the already-traumatized neighborhood kids had to walk past on their way to Belle Harbor School, near Long Island Sound.

The author and her son were talking about how hard it must be for kids in that community to deal with the holidays—on top of everything

else they'd been through—and having to walk by *plane wreckage* every day. The ten-year-old said, "I wish we could do something nice for them, to let them know we're thinking about them." And the rest is a testament to teachers and kids on two sides of a grieving nation.

Alik Crockett (the ten-year-old) and his mom asked his sixth grade teacher if their class could become "penpals" with the kids at Belle Harbor School. Over the Christmas holidays, the new principal of the Long Island school was contacted, and she was thrilled with the idea. When everyone came back from vacation, Alik's class had a mission, one that would go from Suquamish Elementary, on a reservation on Puget Sound, to Belle Harbor Elementary, on Long Island Sound. The project was called "SOUND 2 SOUND, HEART 2 HEART."

The sixth grade teacher in Suquamish, outside Seattle, Mrs. Andrea Neault, showed her students the news coverage of the crash near the New York school and talked about ways to reach out to other

PAUSE

kids. The kids in New York had just finished a unit studying "Indian Culture," in teacher Ron Gerson's class, but knew nothing of how contemporary Native American kids lived. Gerson and Neault made sure that every student got a name of a penpal of his or her own and communications began.

The kids from New York wanted to know what it was like to live "on the rez" and whether or not the kids at Suquamish Elementary lived in "tee-pees." They wanted to know if tribal kids still went down to the water and speared dinner. The letters were honest and inquisitive, but it was astonishing to the kids in Suquamish that there were people who had *never even seen* a *"real" Native American*, let alone had the chance to know one. They were amazed that people on the East Coast would think they were still living as they had in the hey-day of the "Wild West."

So the letters, in packages with art work, flew back and forth and soon the kids all found out that they were much more alike than they were different. Video games, TV, basketball, and music were the big links. They shared what they did after school, what movies they wanted to see, what their families and pets were like, and the details of the two school dances that were about to take place.

It was a terrific experience all around, wonderful in the best sense of the word. The kids ended the school year by sending each other's class pictures, and the teachers stayed in touch, using e-mail for student correspondence the following year. It was just that simple—kids reached out to one another with some compassion, and decades of stereotyping and ignorance went into the "permanent circular file."

Perhaps if we truly appreciated what it means to be a member of a tribe, we would look differently at the world. Tribes are not only for Native Americans, but for any group linked by culture and family. The Celts (Irish) are tribal, as are the Gauls (French). The people of the Middle East and Afghanistan are tribal. Could we have averted some of the tragedy in that part of the planet if the leader of the free world knew that there were different types of Muslims? Different tribes? Would we better understand Africa if we had a better sense of its tribal communities and nations?

> Motherhood is a great
> preparation for national policy.
> Environmental problems? We need to
> say the same things we tell our kids:
> Clean up your mess. Arab-Israeli conflicts?
> Hey! Stop hitting each other!
> Winona La Duke, Native American activist,
> Cofounder of the Indigenous Women's
> Network and Green Party Vice Presidential
> candidate, as interviewed by the author,
> Fall 2000

Since 2001, school districts in Washington State and other places have reached out to tornado and tsunami victims and especially to the kids who had to be relocated after the hurricanes hit the Gulf. Elsewhere, a group of students pulled together evening dresses and tuxes so that kids in one Gulf Coast high school could have their prom. Kids have big hearts and boundless energy, and for most of them, the word "impossible" is only part of a movie title (as in *Mission Impossible*). There were hundreds of spontaneous acts of remarkable kindness.

Kids see what's possible, and they make it happen.

The downside of terrorist acts, tsunamis, African famine, and failed levees has played out in an endlessly recycled tape loop, again and again. But the pictures of struggling children inspired some terrific projects connecting kids, heart to heart. Look at children's artwork after 9/11. Check out the artwork by children who survived Hurricane Katrina and the Gulf Coast flooding. Sure, TV had shown the horror, and some of the kids' drawings depict floating bodies and crying siblings. But TV had been part of the healing, too, and those drawings also show blue skies, brave rescuers—and a rainbow.

Makani Thema-Nixon, Executive Director of The Praxis Project, a media policy and advocacy organization in Washington, D.C., eloquently addresses needs for changes in coverage of social justice issues. Clearly, the rebound of New Orleans will include a variety of those. "Our job as progressives is to expose patterns and systems of injustice in ways that help people understand the structural roots of these issues and shift blame away from victims."

Why are things the way they are? And how can they be different? Among the questions she feels every advocate should ask are:

- Who benefits from unfair policies?
- Who is harmed?
- Who has power?
- Who is left out?

As the Gulf Coast recovers from America's greatest natural disaster, it's vital to "reinforce the people's dream of something better." Access to opportunity will be in a media spotlight like never before.

> We have to develop
> and nurture an infrastructure
> for media—data, sources, and
> studies that document the problems
> and their root causes, and other
> resources to help shift the lens back
> from old stereotypes and victim-blaming,
> and illustrate the "landscape" stories we
> must tell.
> Makani Themba-Nixon
> Executive Director, The
> Praxis Project

ZAP

1. Celebrate your child's family tree. As kids learn more about where they come from, they develop a better picture of who they are. See how far back you can trace your family (there are some great Web sites that make geneology fun.) If you have adopted kids (the author has two), research the places the bio-parents are from and answer questions honestly. Admit when the answer is "I don't know." Silence isn't positive. Exploration is.

2. Take a look at your circle of family friends, and see how you can widen it. Travel—near or far—is a great way to do that. It's as easy as taking a bus to a different library or discovering a new playground or restaurant.

3. Rent *Yesterday,* an HBO film about an African girl who loses her parents to AIDS. (Reading the simple subtitles does not detract from the strength of this film.) *Rabbit-Proof Fence* and *Whale Rider* are additional films that teach strength and celebrate diversity. In fact, Australian Children's Television has an exceptionally good collection of DVDs and video-tapes—the most recent offering is about the e-mails between a boy in London and a girl in Australia, *Noah and Saskia,* enhanced by great post-production work and special effects. Visit the Australian Children's Television Foundation at **www.actf.com.au**. PBS's *Matters of Race,* which explores the complexity of race relations in the United States, is another powerful choice.

How is your ethnic group portrayed?
People being people. Ohi-ti-ka, grade 6
Smart and helpful. Karissa, grade 4
Drunk. Derrick, grade 3

STEREO(TYPES)

You've got to be taught to hate and fear, It's got to be drummed in your dear little ear… You've got to be taught, before it's too late. Before you are six, or seven, or eight, To hate all the people your relatives hate, You've got to be carefully taught!

"Carefully Taught," from the Rogers and Hammerstein musical, South Pacific

"Don't teach your children to hate. Let them pick it up on their own. Like you did." Actor Rob Lowe, satirizing NBC's public service announcement series, *The More You Know*, in a spoof called "For All You Know," 2005

Well, it's true. Unfortunately, kids don't come up with stereotypes on their own. They learn them.

You see, *The Others* isn't just a ghost story with English accents. It's how stereotypes begin. For some people, bias begins with assumptions about the way "they" act, think, or behave. And television, sadly, has reinforced just about every negative stereotype there is. Bias can become bigotry. And when that happens, everybody loses.

We are afraid of "the others"—no matter who they are. And the combination of fear and ignorance (being scared by the unfamiliar or different) is at the root of many conflicts, from the playground sandbox to, well, the larger Sand Box in the Middle East.

TV stereotypes can emerge from a variety of situations, although some may have changed over time. We no longer think *Father Knows Best*,

or that threats of physical spousal abuse, like those in *The Honeymooners,* are worthy of laughter (although, to the great surprise of this TV critic, there are still some who find it hysterical).

The post-WWII, *Leave It To Beaver/Ozzie and Harriet* paradigm of American family life evolved at a glacial rate into depictions of families headed by single parents, (*My Three Sons, The Partridge Family,*) and then went back again to married, LARGE families (*The Brady Bunch, Eight is Enough, Seventh Heaven.*) *The Cosby Show* and *Fresh Prince of Bel-Air* were centered on the lives of black professionals (doctors, lawyers, judges) and often offered guest appearances by critically acclaimed minority actors (Chita Rivera, Ossie Davis, Ruby Dee.) These gave way to more contemporary portrayals of black family life (*Moesha*) and started featuring brown families (*George Lopez*) and Latin story lines. But these shows all have one thing in common: They are situation comedies, or "sit-coms."

Television Week's Lillian Jackson, who writes a column called "Diversity Detail," speaks eloquently about the lack of a plan for genuinely diversifying TV.

> "I think there is a disconnect between the industry and the simmering dissatisfaction among the audience of ethnic minorities, disabled people, and gays and lesbians. I encounter it constantly as I do research for this column.
>
> When I mention to people that I write a column on diversity in television, without my asking, they talk about how they're frustrated by the limited choices. Asians, blacks, and Latinos I speak to complain about the scarcity of programming and **the frequency of stereotypical casting as criminals, clowns, or domestic servants.**
>
> People are disillusioned with the prospects for change…some people cite programs like *The Boondocks* (Cartoon Network) and *Mind of Mencia* (Comedy Central) as positive signs, but are the few cable entries really progress?"

The POWER chapter mentions the recent merger of two networks which feature predominantly minority-oriented programming: UPN (United Paramount Network) and the WB (Warner Brothers). They have become a single entity, the CW (CBS/Warner Brothers, NOT "country western"!). The merger, which officially went on-air in September 2006, has some industry critics concerned. Jackson writes:

> "Will it be another incidence of a fledgling broadcast network (UPN) building itself on the strength of the African American audience, and then abandoning that audience without so much as a backward glance?"

Lillian Jackson also shares her viewing experience as a dormitory resident assistant, years ago:

> "I was den mother to roughly twenty-five young women, among whom I was the only African American. One afternoon, I dropped in on a group of my residents while they were watching TV—*The Jeffersons*. As I entered the room, one girl piped up, "Hey, Lil, we're watching one of **your** shows!" It was meant to be funny, and it was; we all laughed. But here it is 2006, decades later, and broadcast viewing is still greatly divided between yours, mine, and theirs. And 'mine' is almost exclusively sitcoms."

She quotes the often-heard comment that TV is only motivated by one color: GREEN.

> "...that is a trick of smoke and mirrors to obscure the fact that, every TV season, mainstream dramas like *The Book of Daniel*, *Just Legal*, and *Head Cases* become costly cancellations, but their failures don't prevent the appearance of more costly untried mainstream dramas the next season.
>
> I suspect these excuses protect the status quo. After all, if more programs are about people of color, then there will likely be more writers and actors of color and ultimately more network executives of color, which means fewer places for white writers, actors, and executives."

So she has an innovative prescription for what ails TV in the Department of Diversity.

> "...if programming is truly a crapshoot, why not take a chance on something different? Here's a plan: for one year, every broadcast network sets aside one hour a day of prime time and one hour a day of daytime for programming BY and ABOUT people

of color, the disabled, or the LGBT (Lesbian, Gay, Bisexual, Transgender) community. To fill those two daily hours, networks would be forced to seek out **content beyond the comical or criminal**. (Italics by the author.) I think viewers would tune in during these hours, if just to see what the experiment produces."

She's right! But Lillian Jackson knows that the chances of any network's parting with an experimental hour of prime time or daytime is about as likely as Reverend Pat Robertson's doing a cameo appearance on *Queer Eye for the Straight Guy* or acting as the presiding minister at a wedding on *The L Word*. However, Jackson is correct to think that it will take "a radical idea" to "wake up the industry to the fact that change is necessary and unavoidable." And long overdue.

As more diverse writers are hired, the stereotypical characters will be replaced with ones that better reflect the **realities of minority community life**.

Take a look at the stereotypes TV has presented to your kids, and see if they make judgments and generalizations on groups of people, based on how they look, who they hang with, who their family members are, ethnicity, nationality, what events they go to, who and how they worship, how they speak, and how they view the world.

Why is this important? Because people are quite capable of letting their biases erupt into bullying. You would have a better chance of counting sea shells on a beach than the number of arguments, fistfights, and even killings that result from biases that turn to hatred. (See chapter "Volume of Violence.")

To its credit, TV has addressed some of these issues, as well. A PBS documentary by Stanley Nelson, *The Murder of Emmett Till*, about the unsolved death of a young black man, made such an impact on the audience that half a million postcards and letters were sent to the jurisdiction where the murder originally was committed, nearly half a century ago. The result? Thanks to the viewers of the documentary, the murder investigation has been reopened. Emmitt Till's mother may yet live to see justice for the people who butchered her son for "looking at a white woman." The murder of a young gay man in Wyoming

was documented in *The Laramie Project*, which inspired Tony Kushner's play *Angels in America*. The plight of African American men who were used as guinea pigs in government-sponsored biological experiments in the 1940s was finally told through the eyes of the nurse who cared for them in *Miss Evers' Boys* (HBO, 1997). The week of the debut of *Walkout*, an HBO production based on the 1968 school walkout by the Latino community in Los Angeles, minority students—not just Latinos, but Native Americans, Asians,

> Sign seen by Anna Quindlen in
> *Newsweek*, read:
> **We are ALL immigrants. Some of us
> just got here sooner.**

bi-racial kids, and white students, too, in solidarity—took to the streets in a walkout as well. They protested a proposed revision of immigration laws that appeared to many to be discriminatory, and which labeled undocumented workers as "illegals." One sign read: "We are immigrants. WE ARE NOT CRIMINALS."

The Paper Clip Project

Our kids have a pretty good grasp of numbers, but some are just too big to register. Teachers who try to explain "millions"—let alone billions—have a sizeable challenge ahead of them.

In 1998, David Smith (history teacher, football coach, and assistant principal) suggested to the principal, Linda Hooper, that they could use the Holocaust as the basis for teaching tolerance as a volunteer after-school program. They decided to pick a simple object to demonstrate just how many six million actually was.

Whitwell, Tennessee, would not have been anyone's guess for a project teaching diversity and justice. It is 97.35 percent white.

SPONGEHEADZ: U & MEdia

Whitwell is located forty miles away from the courthouse where, in 1925, a teacher was convicted during the "Scopes Monkey Trial" for teaching evolution. It is one hundred miles from Pulaski, the alleged birthplace of the Ku Klux Klan.

Whitwell Middle School housed 425 students. The student body reflected the ethnic make-up of the community, and was mostly white and Christian, with five African-American students and one Latino student. In fact, when the project began, there were no Jewish children in the entire school, and no people in the town personally connected to the Holocaust or related to its survivors. Like many schools removed from urban centers, diversity was a concept, not a reality.

The students simply could not believe that six million people were murdered and that no one did anything to stop it. The eighth grade project's goal, according to their Web site, was to learn "how prejudice and power in the wrong hands can be catastrophic." Six million people being killed because they were "different"? Unthinkable.

And the idea of collecting one paper clip for each victim of the Holocaust was born.

The participants, according to the Whitwell Web site, "...chose paper clips for a special reason. During World War II, Norwegians wore paper clips on their clothes to show their opposition to Nazism and anti-Semitism."

They decided to put out the word that they were collecting six million paper clips and hoped to build a sculpture as a lasting memorial to the estimated six million Jews who were killed between 1939 and 1945, under the authority of the Nazi government and Adolf Hitler.

It didn't matter how many paper clips were donated by any one person at any time. Every single one would be counted individually. Each one represented a human life, and *every single one mattered.*

As the paper clips began arriving, so did letters from Holocaust survivors, offering not only encouragement to the kids in the project, but personal stories of great loss and greater courage. In the beginning, the paper clip collection grew slowly. But two journalists, Peter and Dagmar Schroeder, who were born in Germany during World War II, wrote some articles and published a book about the project, and in April of 2001, the *Washington Post* ran an article on the students' efforts. Soon, paper clips were arriving, not by the tens, or hundreds, but by the thousands.

The idea of a memorial sculpture created by melting the paperclips, to reflect the horrors of the crematorium was replaced by the idea of finding an actual train car that had been used to transport people to the Nazi concentration camps, and to fill it with paperclips for all of the victims of the Holocaust. The Schroeders were instrumental in locating a rail car of that time period. It was shipped to Whitwell and arrived **September 12, 2001.**

A lesson in tolerance had taken on a whole new meaning.

By 2004, the kids had collected thirty million paper clips. There are eleven million in the rail car—for the six million Jews plus five million other victims, including homosexuals, gypsies, and Jehovah's Witnesses, all nominated for extinction in one of the darkest times of human civilization.

It began as a lesson about prejudice.
What happened was a miracle.
Slogan on the poster for the documentary
Paper Clips, 2004

The award-winning documentary about the Paper Clip Project, **Paper Clips,** from Miramax Studios, is must-see TV. For more information, see Wikipedia, where much of the information here was originally found.

You don't have to cross an ocean to find intolerance—but a pretty fair argument could be made that the reason most immigrants came here was to escape it.

There have been several holocausts on our troubled planet, and in fact, in older, worse times, two holocausts were occurring simultaneously: one on the European continent, in which half a million women were burned as witches during the Spanish Inquisition and the Dark Ages that preceded them, a four-hundred-year extermination campaign. The second simultaneous holocaust was taking place on the other side of the planet, in the Americas, where indigenous people in the Northern and Southern hemispheres were forced into slavery and slaughtered for their natural resources. Elsewhere, Muslims were slaughtered by Crusaders and vice-versa. Catholics and Protestants spilled each other's blood. Global history is filled with examples of the failures of human interaction. (Even as this book goes to print, Israel, Lebanon, and much of the region have erupted into a new chapter of their centuries of conflict, while the African continent deals with famine in Darfur and a host of other places. There is widespread political unrest on just about every continent.)

Entire civilizations disappeared after what is now called "First Contact." Record-keeping wasn't as accurate as it is now, but the Mayans and Incas lost numbers in the tens of thousands, sometimes in less than a month's time, according to some documentation kept by European military and Catholic Church officials.

Indigenous people on the North American continent were thought to have numbered about thirty million when what became America was "discovered." There are barely half a million Native Americans left in the United States, and many tribes have become "extinct" through intermarriage and assimilation, their numbers insufficient to be federally recognized. Some "killers" are still in play today: poverty and disease, with alcoholism, meth addiction, and diabetes topping a growing list.

In the twentieth century, in addition to two world wars, we saw the Holocaust in Europe, territorial wars in Africa, Tibetans slaughtered by Chinese, Japanese by Koreans, the people of India subjugated by British, black South Africans by white Boers, Cambodians by Pol Pot's followers, and genocide in Rwanda. This is an incomplete list, but if you were to line up a "biggest hits" marathon on the History Channel, we'd need to put lithium in the entire US water supply.

Tolerance.org

All the more reason for a site like this one, since the following statistics are so appalling:

> Every hour, someone in the United States commits a hate crime.

> Every day, at least eight blacks, three whites, three gays, three Jews, one Latino, and a combination of an indeterminate number of smaller minority groups such as Sikhs, Native Americans, Asians, and Muslims, become victims of hate crimes.

> Every week a cross is burned outside an American home.

> According to FBI statistics, the greatest growth in hate crimes in the new century is against Asian Americans, the LGBT community (lesbian, gay, bisexual, and transgender) and, since 9/11, any people perceived as "Arabic." Most hate crimes are committed in the North and West. (The South no longer holds the lead, as it did during the civil rights movement.)

Tolerance.org, a Web project of the Southern Poverty Law Center, offers ten ways to fight hate. Keep this list near your TV, and when you see or read a story about hate crime, talk with your kids about the story. Don't get mad. Get busy.

Here are the ten tips:

1. **ACT.** Do something. In the face of hatred, apathy will be interpreted as acceptance by the perpetrators, the public, and, worse, the victims. Decent people must take action. If we don't, hate persists.

2. **UNITE**. Call a friend or co-worker. Create a diverse coalition that includes children, police, media, teachers, churches, clubs, and civic organizations. Meet informally at first. Organize a group viewing of the PBS video *Not in Our Town*.

3. **SUPPORT THE VICTIMS.** Let victims know you care. Surround them with comfort and protection. Victims of hate crimes feel terribly alone and afraid, because they have been attacked for simply being who they are—their skin color, their ethnicity, their sexual orientation. Silence AMPLIFIES their isolation and tacitly condones the act of hate. Small acts of kindness—a phone call, a letter—go a long way towards helping and healing.

4. **DO YOUR HOMEWORK.** Understand the difference between a hate crime and a bias incident. Hate groups—and there are more than 750 of them being tracked by the Southern Poverty Law Center in this country—have some common denominators. They are upset by the possibility that a growing immigrant population will make whites a minority in this century. They spread fears of losing control of America to a One World Government dominated by Jewish bankers, multinational corporations, and the United Nations. More often than not, members of hate groups blame scapegoats for their personal failures, low self-esteem, anger, and frustration. They frequently act under the influence of alcohol or drugs, recruiting disaffected, at-risk teens through music and other means.

Though each group has its code words, they tend to share five particular views:

• They want to limit the rights of certain groups.

• They want to divide society along racial, ethnic, or religious lines.

• They believe in conspiracy theories.

• They try to silence any opposition.

• They are anti-government and fundamentalist.

Remember: Most hate crimes are not committed by members of hate groups, but by freelance perps, typically young male thrill-seekers defending turf or looking for people on whom to blame their personal problems. Rarely do they act from deeply held ideologies—they attack targeted groups randomly, choosing whoever is convenient. While these young men act independently, they are fueled by rhetoric from hate groups that dehumanizes their victims—a toxic mix of language, stereotypes, and cultural violence.

5. **CREATE AN ALTERNATIVE.** Never attend a hate rally. Hold an alternative event at the same time, some distance away, to demonstrate unity, strength, tolerance, and nonviolence.

6. **SPEAK UP.** Hate needs to be exposed and denounced. Help news organizations achieve balance and depth, and speak up in ways that are organized, reasonable, and draw people's attention toward unity and tolerance, rather than hate. An informed and unified community is the best defense against hate. Use fliers, bulletins, neighborhood newspapers, letters to the editors, and print advertisements. HATE SHRIVELS UNDER STRONG LIGHT, because underneath the hard-ass rhetoric, most hate purveyors are cowards with low self-esteem, and many will slink away from public ostracism and public pressure.

7. **LOBBY LEADERS.** Cultivate allies in high and visible places; form relationships with community leaders **before** an incident happens. Educate those leaders about the impact of hate, and the root causes of intolerance, so their response can match the incident if one occurs. Demand a quick and serious response. Demand a strong public statement by political leaders. Encourage community leaders to call the incident what it is—a hate crime. Above all, get together and LOBBY FOR ACTION. Make your community leaders walk the walk as well as talk the talk.

8. **LOOK LONG-RANGE.** Hate doesn't do "long distance calls." It often begins near home, in communities where people feel powerless or voiceless, communities in which differences are a cause of fear instead of celebration.

9. **TEACH TOLERANCE.** Bias is learned in childhood. By age three, kids can be aware of racial differences and already verbalize that "white" is more desirable than other colors. By age twelve, they may have some pretty ingrained stereotypes about ethnic, racial, and religious groups. Because stereotypes underlie hate, and almost all hate crimes are committed by guys under the age of twenty, tolerance education is CRITICAL. (See "In The Classroom" at **www.tolerance.org**)

10. **DIG DEEPER.** Tolerance is a personal decision. It comes from an attitude that says that every voice matters, that all people

are valuable, and that no one is "less than." We all have the power to face our own prejudices. (And we all have them!)

> "The best cure for hate is a tolerant, united community. A united coalition is like Teflon. Hate can't stick there."
> Chris Bucher, of Yulon, Pennsylvania, Quoted by the study

Ask yourself: Am I quick to label people as "rednecks" or "illegals"? Do I tell gay jokes? Do I put down people who have money problems, rather than trying to understand what's going on in their lives? Do I let people around me make sexist or racist jokes? Do I get information about people from other cultures from members of those cultures or from what someone else says about them? Do I listen and learn when people share their experiences? How often am I in the minority, and *what does that feel like?*

Consider the remarks of Senator George Allen (R-VA), who, in August 2006, addressed a videographer for the opposition, a person of color, as "macaca."

At a relatively small campaign stop, in front of less than one hundred people, Allen pointed out the dark-skinned man, saying, "Let's welcome macaca, or whatever your name is…" and used the term a number of times.

The problem is that the young videographer, S. R. Sidarth, didn't need to be "welcomed" to the state. Unlike Senator Allen, he had been *born in Virginia.* He was astonished that a sitting U.S. Senator **would use a racial slur for cheap laughs—at an all-white campaign stop**.

Video of the event was posted immediately, and quickly became a national news item.

"Macaca" derives from the word "macaque," a type of monkey. But many Europeans know the word as a slam against people of color, similar to referring to African Americans as "monkeys." (Some people likened it to the n-word.)

Senator Allen's staff, after first asserting that "there was nothing to apologize for," began a series of embarrassing public translations and excuses for the comment. Allen also claimed he had "used a word whose meaning he didn't know," not a ringing endorsement for any politician. What the news media did not report (but the blogosphere did) was that the senator's mother, a French-Tunisian immigrant, would have been very familiar with the term. The senator, who speaks fluent French (also not reported in main-stream media, since anything vaguely French was suspect—think post 9/11 "freedom fries") had to have heard the term since his infancy *and knew exactly what he was saying*.

In previous campaigns, an alleged racial slur by a candidate could easily be denied. But since the video was posted on **www.YouTube.com**, it received millions of hits, and anyone who wanted to see the senator at his condescending best could simply walk to the nearest computer and find it.

Sidarth's family was highly offended, and justifiably so. His outraged grandparents wrote letters to editors of area newspapers, demanding an apology. It took almost two weeks for Senator Allen to phone the student with one. When asked whether or not he thought the senator's apology was sincere, Sidarth said, "No comment."

The story does have a noteworthy ending. When he returned to college for his senior year, Mr. Sidarth wanted to take a particularly crowded media class—people were writing extensive papers just to get into the course. Mr. Sidarth's course application document contained only three words: "I am macaca."

He got in.

The latest "definition" of "macaca" concentrates on the last two syllables, since apparently, Allen's staff had called the ever-present kid with a camera a "macaca-head." (No translation necessary.) At least, by graduation, Mr. Sidarth will be able to share his part in a media phenomenon which illustrates the best way to combat prejudice: to expose it. In the process, he may have derailed the presidential aspirations of a "bubba wannabe"—thanks to TV, the Internet, and a free and independent Fourth Estate.

In the meantime, we can hope that "the distinguished Senator from Virginia" visits **www.tolerance.org** soon. Considering the fact that Senator Allen's career includes stalwart opposition to the holiday honoring Dr. Martin Luther King, and an affinity for Confederate flags, this might be a smart move.

It's a good day for a race. The human race. Bill Ballard, Lakota friend and *Spongeheadz* supporter

No discussion of stereotyping would be complete without a look at gender bias. Fortunately, our children are not as likely to buy into gender stereotyping as much as their parents, grandparents, and great-grandparents did. In fact, in some circles, the failure of the so-called Marriage Amendment in 2006 was attributed to the fact that the children of the people who tried to make it happen didn't think that their choice of a partner was as big a deal as their elders did. As more of these young voters express themselves at the polls, privacy issues are beginning to take precedence over rules set by church and religion. Perhaps there is still hope for separation of church and state—one of the reasons the nation's founders started this country in the first place.

Some of the people waging the gender and cultural wars are about to learn some valuable lessons in maturity—from their kids, of course.

There is a relatively new organization called "See Jane," an outgrowth of "Dads and Daughters," which monitors how girls are portrayed on screen. Their latest report offers some interesting—and predictable—information. The title of their new report says it all: **G Movies Give Boys a D: Portraying Males as Dominant, Disconnected, and Dangerous.**

> **Boys are crazy, girls are smart.**
> Alex, grade 5
> **Girls are weaker than boys.**
> Meagan, grade 4
> **Girls always get saved.**
> Allison, grade 3

Gender portrayals seen in films—which, of course, end up on TV—have a strong impact on children ages birth to eleven, because these children are so impressionable. Entertainment images and stories help influence a child's important developmental task of what it means to be male or female. This is especially true with preschool children, who are having their ideas of manhood and womanhood shaped and integrated into their own personalities. *The images of mainstream media matter because they are important components (along with family, religion, and other factors) in creating the personalities of children who become adult women and men.* Some of the older research from the 70s still holds true, too—"that when young children see someone who looks like them on-screen, but engages in nonstereotypical activities, they are more likely to try out those new activities themselves," says Lawence Cohen, Ph.D., psychologist and author of *Playful Parenting*. To kids who have grown up with female astronauts, Supreme Court justices, senators, doctors, and basketball stars, seeing women in those roles is not unusual—it's a given. Remember, please, that it took the women's movement of the 1970s to bring about even the first of those changes, and TV played a role in that, too.

Two of the most talked about female stereotypes at the moment are "Boss as Bitch" (*The Devil Wears Prada*) and "Big, Bold, and Black" (*Momma's House*).

And the Missing in Action Award goes to the Sunday morning talk shows, which are still mostly male and usually white. *Newsweek*'s Eleanor Clift has been bearing the sister-standard on PBS's *The McLaughlin Group* for two decades (along with Margaret Carlson for a while), occasionally joined by another woman, a guest. **Very** occasionally.

This Week sometimes features "power couple" Jay Carney and news reporter Claire Shipman. Every once in a while James Carville and Mary Matalin, the ultimate political odd couple, do a news show together, when he is not busy with Democratic Party strategy and she can break away from Vice President Cheney's office.

And seeing a news program anchored by two women, instead of two men, was a rarity until recently. However, 2006 marks CBS's first foray into presenting a solo female anchor at 6 p.m. You probably already know her name. (She also writes award-winning children's books.) Katie Couric's newscast on CBS in September 2006 represents another milestone: The network will simulcast *CBS Evening News* live online, the first time any network has done so. (She'll also be on radio and iPods.)

On TV, for the younger set, the overwhelming bad news is that girls, after all this time, are still outnumbered three to one by boys. Most of TV's stories are male-driven, the action is male-driven, and girl characters are still more likely to have scenes involving shopping and other passive, stereotypical activities, or discussions about clothes, hair, and personal grooming products than active action sequences.

A prime-time exception that offered a working mom dealing with her kids (and the world) was *Commander in Chief*, which showed us how a woman in the White House could handle national, global, and even family crises. The founder of **www.SeeJane.org** is Geena Davis— the actor who played the part of that woman prime-time President. The important work being done by SeeJane will no doubt outlast *Commander in Chief*, which, when this book went to print, was, according to the ABC network president, "shelved." But as Commander in Chief of your remote control, you can use the opportunities TV presents to make a contribution to dialogue and understanding.

1. Somewhere near you is an ethnic community. Really! Find it, visit, go out for a meal, and support the neighborhood's economy. Your children need to see as many different kinds of people as possible, so check out everything from Greek Orthodox Church fairs to Lunar New Year in Asian neighborhoods, holy days in the Latin, Italian, and eastern Catholic communities, African American film festivals, celebrations at the local synagogue or mosque, solstice and equinox observances, art exhibits and concerts, and pow-wows over the course of summer months in nearly every tribal community. "Chief Seattle Days," on the chief's home turf in Suquamish, Washington, has three days of traditional dancing and salmon roasting, events, speakers, and crafts vendors. Take a look at your circle of family friends, and see how you can widen it. Travel—near or far—is a great way to do that. It's as easy as taking a bus to a different library, or discovering a new playground or restaurant.

And, once having gone somewhere new for a celebration, GO BACK and walk through the museum, if there is one. You can start with your own lineage and work out in ever-widening circles from there, because, with the exception of the tribes and First Nations, we are all immigrants. (Some of us just got here sooner!)

2. Visit the Tolerance Project at **www.tolerance.org**. Introduce some of the ideas at the site to your family, and share some of the great school activities with your kids' teachers and your friends.

3. Keep track of actors in sit-coms, commercials, documentaries, and action films. Who is missing? Find a "classic" film festival in a particular genre (westerns, war movies, mysteries—even musicals). See how interaction between races was different from the way it is now. Then look for some copies of *I'll Fly Away* or classic civil rights films and documentaries, such as HBO's *Rosa Parks* and *Eyes On the Prize* on PBS, and watch them with your kids. Above all, TALK ABOUT WHAT YOU SEE.

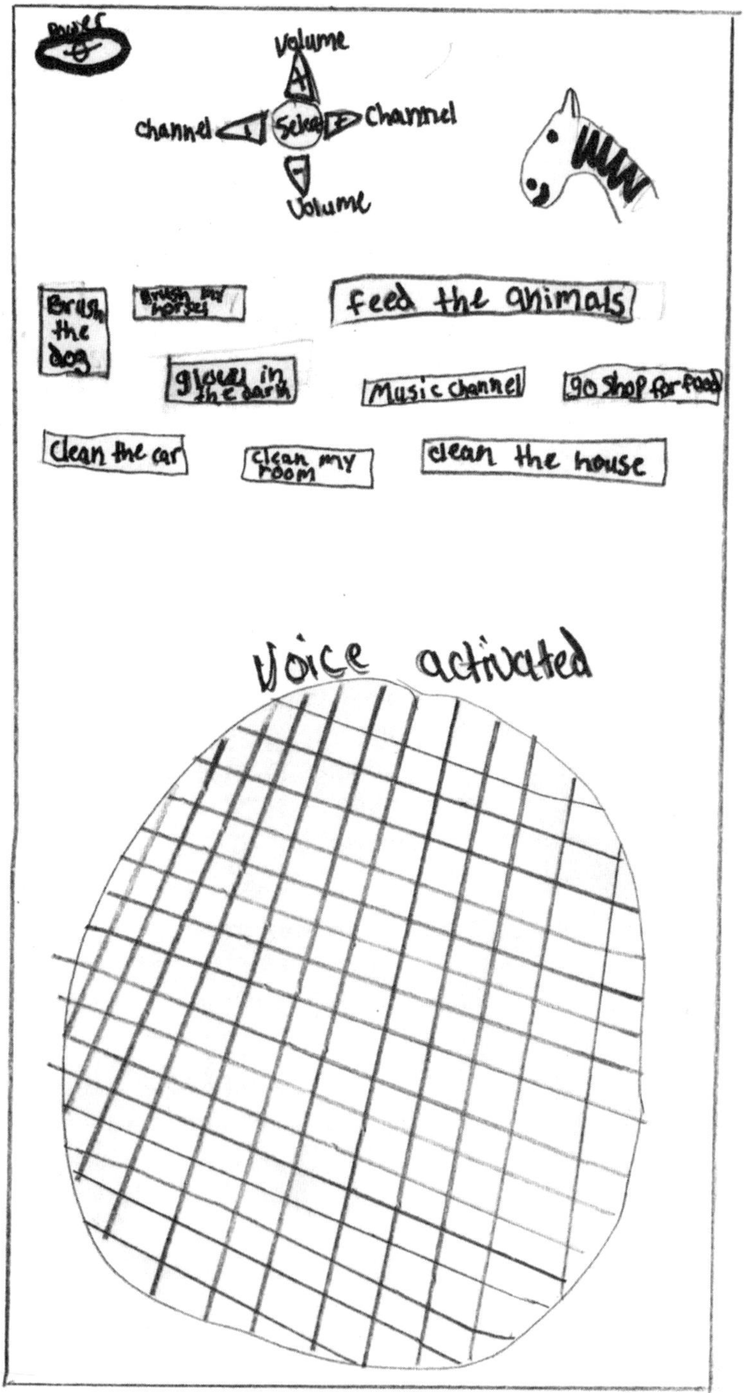

Power

Volume

channel ◁ Select ▷ Channel

Volume

Brush the dog

Brush my horsey

feed the animals

glow in the dark

Music channel

go shop for food

clean the car

clean my room

clean the house

Voice activated

Unsigned

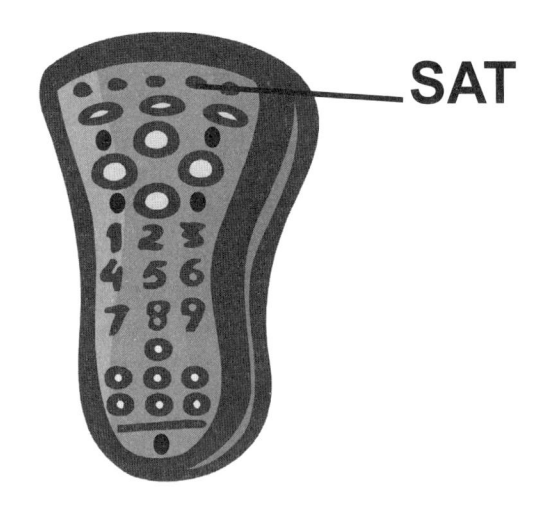

SAT is the past tense of "sit," which is what you used to do in your living room before you became so media savvy. You know, when you just SAT there with your kids and didn't think about what you were watching, or how it got there.

But SAT is also an abbreviation for the way some of us watch TV, as well as the way we transfer information and communicate: by satellite.

Satellites can:

- Make it possible to order pizza from home without using a phone
- Follow a package sent by a friend for your birthday, to see if it will arrive on time
- Enable you to play games with someone on the other side of the planet
- Track a tsunami and warn people to seek higher ground
- See geographic changes after a hurricane
- Show the areas of the rainforest disappearing
- Measure the size of changes in the ice caps
- Keep you from getting lost in your car

And lots of other things as well. Of course, the original intent of satellites was military—to keep the country safe from a nuclear attack. But, as is the case with so many other military inventions, there have been many creative, innovative, and peaceful developments since then.

"We wouldn't need satellites if the world was flat," says one Web site. "We could just send a signal from point A to point B." But since we live on a water-covered ball, that doesn't work.

Here is a very basic illustration of how satellites "work."

Satellites make it possible to hear radio stations from faraway places, and they make it possible for the sounds and images of digital communications to be clearer.

According to *Forbes* magazine, civilian GPS equipment made its debut in the late 1980s, but the Pentagon built in electronic errors to limit the accuracy of nonmilitary devices to within three hundred feet. In 2000, President Bill Clinton ordered those intentional errors—known as "selective availability"—turned off, increasing the accuracy of civilian devices to between thirty and sixty feet. GPS's "golden age" had begun.

Lynn Ziegler

In recent years, electronics wizards have figured out new uses for GPS technology. Here are some of the latest ways GPS is part of your life:

- When integrated into cellular handsets, GPS receivers can alert users to interesting local landmarks.

- They can incorporate real-time traffic updates and reroute you to beat the local bottleneck.

- They can add "geotags" to digital photos, so you know where you took that amazing shot! (For now, it will look like gibberish, like PNTX 564788103107, but within a year or two, it will read Olympic Mountains, October 31, 2007.)

- They track deliveries of many kinds, including furniture, office documents, cargo, and business mail.

- As the technology gets smaller and less expensive, your dog can have a locator in its collar. No more leaflets if the dog is missing—just track him down.

- Mountain-climbers can get GPS devices that will alert search-and-rescue teams when they are in trouble.

- For the hunter or sports-fisherman (and most of the rest of us!): A route-planning feature that will let you know when you will have cell phone service again.

- For bikers: A handle-bar mounted GPS system to monitor your rear-wheel speed—and your heart rate—simultaneously.

- One "family locator" will send out a signal if your child is six blocks away from home instead of three, like you told him to be. (Already available.)

- Tamper-proof ankle tags for sex offenders and prisoners under house arrest.

- Runners: With some software, you can create your own workouts and running areas and analyze your performance once you're done.

- Traveling abroad? One GPS will not only provide foreign roadmaps, but an electronic translator.

SPONGEHEADZ: U & MEdia

📺 Disabled drivers can now enjoy new recreation by going off-roading in a hybrid four-wheeled "wheelchair" vehicle that always lets family members know where they are.

One piece of promotional writing offered this rationale: "if you care about something, you want to know where it is." Other people are less enthusiastic.

It's not always about things.

The upside is that no matter where you are, you can always be found. It's also the downside, because you are technically under surveillance and tracked—by everyone—24/7.

Your children need to understand this. You need to do more than reserve their copies of *1984* and *Brave New World* at your library. Their concept of "Big Brother" should not be limited to who is allowed to stay up later. Planet Earth has a new reality show called "Surveillance World," and we—all six billion of us—are the stars.

ZAP 1. Visit Web sites like **www.howstuffworks.com** and see if you can help your children understand why satellites are so much a part of our daily lives. Ask them what (besides global surveillance) satellites might be used for in the twenty-second century.

2. Visit the NASA Web sites, check out the Mars Rover and the Hubble Telescope, and enjoy some of the zillions of astronomical sites on the Web. Then go to the library or video store for some old-school science fiction movies. Be sure to point out that women in space did not end up wearing short skirts and heels. And that, sometimes, the captain is a woman.

3. Ask your kids how and what they would like to "track" long distance (pets, friends, teams, friends or relatives in the military service, weather.) Then let them do it!

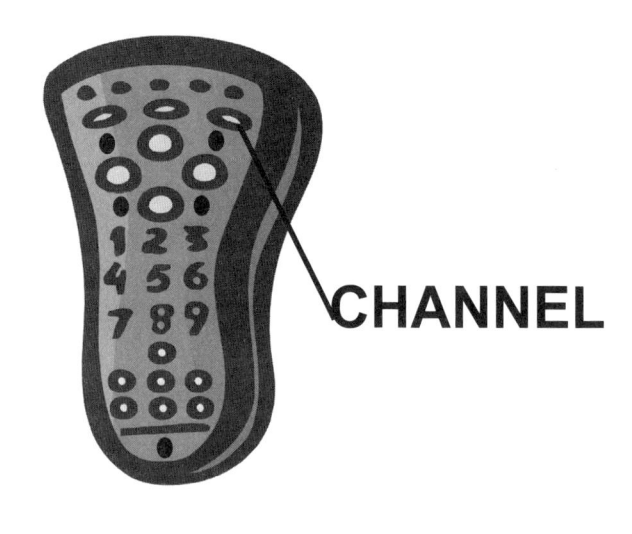

CHANNEL

You know what your channels are. And whether or not your favorites are on broadcast, cable, satellite, or HDTV, you're willing to expend enough energy to find what you want to see. The channel is a conduit between you and what you choose to watch. The best channel becomes your destination. (And you don't need to be a channel surfer if you know where the best airwaves are.)

"Channel" is also a verb.

In an energy-conscious world, we know what it takes to keep the TV on. We also have a tremendous natural resource in the living room: our children's energy.

More importantly, we need to explore what it takes to channel that force, and to keep our children tuned in—to themselves. Kids need to be aware of health issues, especially to counter some (OK, a lot!) of the messages TV cheerfully broadcasts to them every day.

There is real life beyond the living room, and we need to prepare our kids for it.

SPONGEHEADZ: U & MEdia

Here is a quick list of the top ten health issues TV shows are addressing, and why you need to make an effort to find programming and channels that are progressive, intelligent, innovative, and creative.

- OBESITY

- DRINKING (alcohol abuse)

- SMOKING (tobacco abuse)

- METH, INHALANTS, PRESCRIPTION DRUGS (and other substance abuse)

- PERSONAL SAFETY (extreme sports, car racing)

- ENVIRONMENTAL RISKS (climate crisis, unresolved pollution problems)

- SEX (sexuality, sexual orientation, STDs, AIDS, teen pregnancy and prevention, choice, and adoption)

- SUICIDE

- DEATH WITH DIGNITY

- GUNS

2006 brought a new cable program called *Honey, We're Killing Our Kids*. In it, a family with eating problems is recorded going about their daily lives. Then a psychologist steps in and takes pictures of the children, and, in front of the anxious parents, morphs the images into what that child might look like in thirty years, based on his or her current—and dreadful—eating habits. Then, for three weeks, the psychologist and other professionals work with the family to make radical behavioral changes. At the end of the program, the morphing segment is reconfigured, and the kids show a healthier future appearance, with the implication that life will be better and last longer for the children. (The psychologist has gone so far as to say, "Based on our new calculations, you may have added eleven years to your child's life.")

Honey, we're killing our kids, all right, but it's not just with obesity. And a deftly edited, forty-minute turnaround works ONLY on TV—not in real life. The media literacy resources at the end of this book can provide names of programs dealing with all of the issues listed above, many of which are beginning to be dealt with as part of public school health curricula. However, some school districts, like some TV networks, shy away from addressing these issues, and they do so at their peril.

A case in point: In a smallish school district near Seattle, there have been seven suicides in the past five years. All were boys between twelve and seventeen. It was documented that four of the kids who committed suicide had been mocked, bullied, and ostracized, and it's possible that the others had similar experiences at some point before making that terrible decision. To its credit, the school district in question developed a peer counseling group, in which students received training, and then went to talk to kids at other schools. But, clearly, more needs to be done, as the suicides continue.

And it's not just boys. A recent study shows that Latinas in the thirteen to seventeen age range have the highest suicide rate of all teens.

Some of these health issues, and how they are treated in media, are hamstrung by outdated regulations, while in other areas, legislation has not kept pace with scientific research. Some of these subjects raise peoples' blood pressure by their mere mention. But they all deserve some notice and attention, since every one of them has been woven into storylines on TV this year.

It really is as simple as making connections. An issue like stem-cell research, for example, may follow a TV show about young cancer patients. You may want to connect with your local children's hospital about connecting kids (maybe a classroom project?) via-email and visits. Ariel Hellwig, a patient in Children's Hospital and Regional Medical Center, Seattle, Washington, is not only the teen critic for this book, but she intends to spread media literacy around the ward, because **kids in hospitals and long-term care facilities—and at home—watch a lot of TV. Here's to a unique group of future media critics!**

It was announced today that children who watch a lot of television do not develop behavior problems. This, according to a new study in this month's issue of *LAZY PARENTS MAGAZINE.* *Saturday Night Live's* Tina Fey, for Weekend Update

Go back over the ten topics on Page 86, and see if there are resources available to your kids in your area. Find out what the school's policy is about bullying and abusive behavior. Ask if there is a community crisis line, and if there isn't, START ONE!

Programming on these critical issues can also help your children develop **empathy**, a counter to the global health issues that sometimes give older people "disaster fatigue" (Katrina/famine/flood/fire/ etc.). Think of them as emo/media vitamins. The very real damage TV can do to a child's health is to **increase insensitivity** to the plight of others, locally and globally—especially events involving children.

The good news is that a lack of empathy is both preventable and curable. But you have to talk with your children about issues and events.

For additional health information, check out the daily bulletins and excellent reports on health and related media issues at the Kaiser Foundation (**www.kff.org**), which anchored much of the research for this book.

Programs about these health issues can sometimes speak with more eloquence than a parent with an emotional stake, such as the well-being of the "offsprung," in the health issue at hand. A healthy media diet can contribute in to your family's well-being. Urge your local PTA or PTSA to encourage inclusion of a regular column/feature/listing on positive programming in the monthly newsletter. Teachers, especially, will thank you for it.

Now that you're more media savvy, you might even end up writing that item yourself.

ZAP 1. Ask if your child's school has a tobacco prevention program. The best ones use media literacy as a teaching tool, in which kids create their own posters, slogans, and PSAs. In fact, a twelve-year-old British boy created a terrific anti-smoking campaign in the U.K., comparing cigarettes to "Jack the Ripper." Check the "Resources" section for excellent contacts. Of course, if you are a smoking parent, the campaign may have to begin at home.

2. Use sporting events as a way to get kids to notice advertising for alcohol and tobacco. Although advertisements for cigarette companies have been taken off American airwaves, many programs still show people—especially teens—smoking. At Super Bowl time, an excellent program is offered at the ACME Web site (**www.acmecoalition.org**) analyzing TV commercials on the Monday after the Big Game. AME (**www.action4mediaed.org**) breaks down the cost of advertising on NASCAR race cars, and your kids will be challenged to count how many cigarette ads (names and logos) they see in a thirty-second clip. The number will astound you all.

3. Use every opportunity in your neighborhood to connect your child with health issues. If there is a student at school with MS or cancer, use that fact to open some discussions on stem cell research, technology, or alternative medicines. Ask your children to identify places that are in line with ADA (Americans with Disabilities Act) guidelines and to take action when they find venues that aren't. Don't wait until a broken leg puts a family member in a wheelchair, even temporarily. Access is everything!

Finally, if your family has experienced a crisis in one of these health categories, urge your children to deal with it through creative means, like writing (an article, a song, a play, a rap, a eulogy) or creating art. One of the most powerful examples of this kind of thinking was demonstrated when a group of concerned adults used sticks from the debris of Katrina to make and fly kites with children in a Gulf Coast neighborhood. The kids involved in this activity said how good it felt to see each unique kite take off and soar. One participant said, "It felt like hope."

shoot gun

shoot Flaming Match

use Hypno beam

use jump spring

Fly

Summon evil monster

Summon of arms

Activate rockets to bost speed

911 botton

rocket rocket rocket

Derek

"Don't read anything! Not even this."

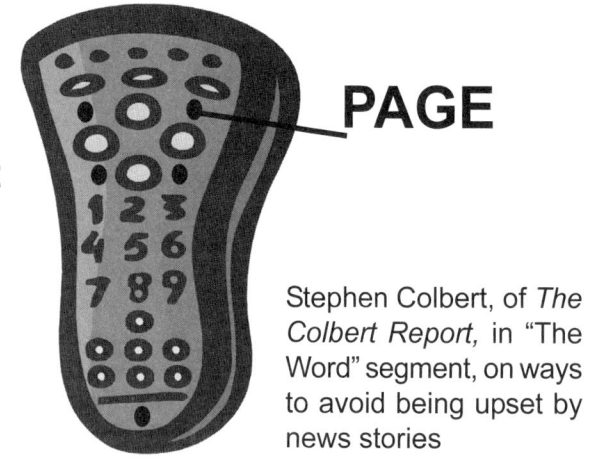

PAGE

Stephen Colbert, of *The Colbert Report,* in "The Word" segment, on ways to avoid being upset by news stories

One of the most important connections you can make between your children and the TV is that of the written word. It's as simple as this: without reading and writing, TV would not be possible. So make the leap—and think of the remote as a library card on AAA batteries. Or mega-vitamins. Or SOLAR PANELS! (But not steroids.)

Great progress has been made in recent years in keeping kids jazzed up about reading. *Reading Rainbow* on PBS still leads the way. The Harry Potter books can be credited with engaging millions of new readers as well. The NBA and the WNBA jumped into reading promotion through PSAs and personal appearances. And, thanks to Oprah Winfrey's famed Book Club, moms, dads, and caregivers began reading more, too. **Oprah Winfrey, with her passion for excellence in the written and spoken word, has created more interest in reading and learning than any single individual on TV, and this nation—this world—owes her a tremendous thank you.**

In the chapter on the MUTE button, a suggestion is made to read the dialogue as it is spoken, using closed captioning. The next step is to remember how much reading is involved in watching TV, and how many great stories can be told on the small screen.

So why not combine the two?

Brij Kothari, the president of Planet Read, is a proponent of same-language subtitling for TV. With a grant from Google, Kothari, a faculty member of the Indian Institute of Management, has made great strides in improving literacy by having children's programming subtitled. And when the characters break into familiar songs, the subtitling highlights words *in different colors*.

Kothari is convinced that the best way to begin this process is by using it with music. In places where this is already being done around the world, literacy rates have shown tremendous improvement. It's being done in Finland, where the subtitling appears automatically, in China, and in numerous other countries.

On average, our children watch at least four hours of TV every day. Can you imagine sending them into the living room to watch shows so that they will become better readers? *Planet Read's* strategy could "save the American educational system," according to Air America's Al Franken. You can find out more at **www.planetread.org** and **www.bookbox.com**.

TV as book box. That's the whole point of the PAGE button!

Kids are sponges, right?
Air America's Al Franken, interviewing Brij Kothari, thanking him for proving his own literacy theory (and the author's)

Almost everything you see on the big screen will eventually be available in your living room, and the time lapse between a film's appearance in a movie theater and your home theatre continues to shrink.

But never let your kids forget about that portable, multi-media, sur-round-sound entertainment system they already have: their imagina-tions. And what engages that better than **WORDS**? Their brains become the SFX generators, and they can voice everything from their own creative centers.

In 2006, the United States has a 14 percent illiteracy rate.

That's a problem. Want to be part of the solution?

LET'S KEEP OUR KIDS READING. Read to them, read with them, let them write their own TV shows or videogames and describe them in excruciatingly painful detail to you—but keep them involved in the creative process of putting one word after another. Show them how much fun it is to imagine their words coming to life. Then help them do it—read their own words back to them. Celebrate their writing and creative projects every way you can.

And speaking of reading… If your child is sucked into advertising for a new cell phone (see next chapter, called "SELECT"), don't despair. At least not yet.

Your kids might just want to check out a book. A whole book. On their cell phone.

In Japan, it is not uncommon now to catch people reading—while they are riding on public transportation, or even waiting for a traffic light to change, **using their cell phones.** As a writer for Associated Press observed, "Your eyes probably hurt just *thinking* about it."

According to an article posted on **www.MSNBC.com**, several mobile Web sites in Japan are offering readers hundreds of novels—clas-sics, best sellers, and some works written *especially for the medium*.

It takes some getting used to, apparently. Only a few lines pop up at a time, because the phone screen is about *half the size of a business card*. But the quality of the liquid crystal display (LCD) and features like automatic page-turning (or scrolling) make it bearable. So now, if you or your children want to read a scary story by Stephen King or watch Harry Potter's wand spark in the dark—you can. As they say in the movies, "Coming soon to a (teeny, tiny) screen near you."

That's not how most of us read.

The decision to take a book out of the library or buy one in a bookstore is not as simple as it once was. So let's talk about the patriots at the front lines of a very important battle: librarians.

Librarians ROCK. They are leading the way in taking an important stand on issues that our children will be dealing with for the rest of their lives: PRIVACY AND INTELLECTUAL FREEDOM. As a parent, you should be concerned by this, and here's why.

More documents have been reclassified as secret since 2001 than in previous decades. Some of these documents, according to the government's own records, may be scheduled to be destroyed. And how will anyone be able to prove that a document in question *ever existed in the first place?*

An informed electorate is the only way a democracy truly lives up to its name. And the importance of reading that information is the whole point of this chapter.

So it should disturb and distress you that, in the awful days after the worst and first terrorist attack on continental American soil in the twentieth century, laws were enacted and voted on by some people WHO DIDN'T READ THEM FIRST. The law is called "The USA PATRIOT Act."

The USA PATRIOT Act has nothing to do with being a patriot. It is an acronym for **U**niting and **S**trengthening **A**merica by **P**roviding **A**ppropriate **T**ools **R**equired to **I**ntercept and **O**bstruct **T**errorism Act. But by using that acronym, it implies that people who do not like some provisions of this law are "unpatriotic."

Just forty-five days after September 11, with almost no debate, Congress passed this flawed piece of legislation, and it was quickly signed and enacted into law. Some of the lawmakers did not receive a copy of the law until five hours before they voted on it. Some members of Congress openly admit to not having read the entire text (over one thousand pages of it). The document discussed on the eve of the vote was also amended in key areas, and thus was different from the version lawmakers had briefly discussed that day.

The USA PATRIOT Act gives the government the power to access your medical records, your tax records, and information about the books you buy or borrow—without probable cause. It also gives government the power to break into your home and conduct secret searches without telling you for weeks or months. Indefinitely. Maybe ever.

Librarians, booksellers, and concerned voters lobbied hard to get the USA PATRIOT Act changed when it came up for renewal in 2005, but it was renewed for another four-year term. Many people still feel that portions of the law limit First Amendment rights in significant areas, including whether or not librarians and booksellers can be forced to hand over to the government the lists of books you have read and/or ordered. Some librarians in California simply shredded the daily logs to protect library patrons' privacy. In Connecticut, four librarians went to court to fight the legislation, but were prevented by a gag order from talking about their problems with the law. That gag order was lifted only when the PATRIOT Act was renewed for another four years.

So, when you go to the library to read about something you've seen on TV or to a bookstore for some research material, be sure to make an effort to thank the librarian and the bookseller for defending the Constitution, the Bill of Rights, and your intellectual freedom. You'll make their day.

Don't put brakes on your child's curiosity. Whatever they ask, encourage them to

READ ALL ABOUT IT!

1. Read the Bill of Rights with your kids. Explain them as a "top ten list" that helps government work better for the people.

2. Look for screenplays of your child's favorite movies, and read along with the film. See if the stage directions match!

3. Look at the work done by Books Not Bars, a coalition housed at the Ella Baker Center for Human Rights. The Oakland, California, group works for radical change in the juvenile justice system, which, for the record, is filled with kids who have reading problems. The project has won recognition for reminding the public of the need for opportunity for thousands of young people who deserved much better.

Books change lives!

Don't wait for your school, your state, or your country to apply the lessons of Planet Read. Tell your children that they already live there.

NOTE: NBC has linked up with Scholastic to restock Gulf Coast state libraries, and other large corporations are also part of that effort. Thank you for doing your part, too: A portion of every sale of *SPONGEHEADZ: U & MEdia* goes to replace books lost in the Gulf Coast disaster.

One last and lasting suggestion: Instead of sending flowers to a funeral, donate a book in the departed's name to a local library. Send the family a note with the book title and the library it was given to. This will be especially meaningful if the friend or relative was an avid reader or an educator. You will create a living, unforgettable memorial to that special person.

SELECT

"The accusation that TV news has a political agenda misses the point—it is not partisanship,

but profitability that shapes what you see."

Ted Koppel, *New York Times* Editorial, 1.29.06

"Pervasive and powerful, advertising's effects largely go unseen, because *we think about advertising like fish think about water*—we don't." Roy Fox, Professor of Education University of Missouri, Columbia

You don't need to be told about commercials on our airwaves. We are all swimming in them. No button on the remote control is more aptly named than this one.

Advertising breaks down into some very basic categories:

Stuff we eat.

Stuff we think we need to have a healthy, sustainable life.

Everything else.

STUFF WE EAT: THEORETICALLY, FOOD

Food advertising is different from any other kind of promotional work. We can *choose* to invest in technology, clothing, trips, education, toys, books, cars—the list is endless. But everybody has to eat.

Before you read any further, run, do not walk, to a local bookstore (or go online) and pick up two books. The first is *Consuming Kids: Protecting Our Children from the Onslaught of Marketing and Advertising,* by Susan Linn, Ph.D. The other book is *Born To Buy*, by Juliet Schor.

Dr. Linn and Dr. Alvin Poussaint (a consultant to *Sesame Street, The Cosby Show*, and other favorites) are co-founders of the Campaign for a Commercial-Free Childhood, a nonprofit organization of determined activists in Boston. They operate out of the Judge Baker Children's Center and are affiliated with Harvard—as well as with some impressive national success stories. They are working to take that very large collection of concentric circles off the backs of our children, who are targeted by marketers 24/7. Some marketers refer to the market potential of selling to children as "cradle to grave." Or womb to tomb.

> They don't hold office,
> they can't vote, and most of them
> don't have much money, but kids have
> become a key constituency in media policy
> in Washington.
> Paige Albiniak
> Broadcasting and Cable

"Advertising is trickier than ever," Albiniak writes. That's true. It's also trickier for the advertisers, because they are navigating new laws and facing new challenges from media-literate parents like you! As they say in Australia, where children's television is some of the best in the world, *"GOOD ON YA!"*

For our kids, advertising is part of their environment, in and out of home, school, and just about everywhere else. We need to show kids just how tricky the advertising game is, and teach them how to **take every message and shred it so they know what's inside**.

The New Mexico Media Literacy Project offers five "Ad Deconstruction Tips" used by this billion-dollar industry that targets our kids.

1. Identify and show your kids how these visual images, symbols, and simple techniques of persuasion work. NMMLP provided the list, and the author is providing the examples:

   Flattery - Buying this product says nice things about you.

   Humor - (Especially if you're new to this planet, for example.)

   Hyperbole - Over the top adjectives—it's the best, most super-fab item in the whole, wide world!

   Use of power words - Strong, unstoppable, manly. Think Hummer ads.

   Distortions of fact - Parents can call these what they are: lies.

   Repetition - "I want my babyback, babyback, babyback......ribs." Or

   "HEAD ON. Apply directly to the forehead!

   　　HEAD ON. Apply directly to the forehead!

   　　　　HEAD ON. Apply directly to the forehead!"

   Testimonial - "You'll jump as high as _____ of the NBA!!!"

   Name Calling - No one will say "You have gross, coffee-stained teeth" again.

   Simplification - Because it's for *you*.

   Appeals to "scientific evidence" - "In the latest double-blind study, patients lost six pounds the first week...."

   Nostalgia - "Remember the good old days? When…"

   Bandwagon - "Everybody's got one of the new_____. You've GOTTA have one too!"

2. Techno Effects and Subliminal Images:
   How is the scene framed?
   What camera angles and lighting techniques are used?
   Where is the viewer positioned?
   What DFX (digital effects) are used?
   What kind of music is used? How loud is it?
   How do all of these effects contribute to the power of the ad?

3. Emotions and the Story:
   What story is the ad trying to tell you?
   What "problems" will the product solve?
   What associations does the ad make with the product? (Sexy, cool, athletic, etc.)
   Who are the advertisers trying to get you to believe?
   What's the message?
   What emotions does the ad appeal to?
   What is the logic behind the ad?

4. Intended and Unintended Effects:
   Who is the target audience for the ad?
   How do you know?
   What are some ways other audiences might respond to the ad?
   What meanings could different audiences infer from the ad?

5. Identify the Marketing Strategy of the Ad
   How long is this ad?
   How long has it been running?
   What does the advertiser hope the ad will do for their public relations or product image?

You're probably thinking you can't keep this info in your head as a commercial streaks by. Don't "misunderestimate" yourself. The tips break down to five easy questions:

1. What is it and how are they selling it?

2. How does it look?

3. How does it grab you?

4. Are they getting to you?

5. Are you going to buy it?

That last one is the most important. Did you SELECT their product?

Now that you know how to break down an ad, let's take a closer look at the marketing you and your kids have survived until now. Perhaps you feel you've been manipulated. You're right. You have been. Not any more!

Let's start with the youngest consumers, the ones who haven't been born yet. Marketing to moms-to-be includes CDs, in-utero-read-aloud material, and music to create healthy, smart babies. Once the baby arrives, then you can start playing the DVDs and CDs designed to reinforce the fact that: **a**) s/he is a genius, and **b**) s/he's going to Harvard. (These products are actually called *Baby Einstein, Bee Smart, etc.)*

You can thank the author now for saving you more than the cost of this book. NONE OF THE "SMART BABY" PRODUCTS WILL MAKE ANY DIFFERENCE IN YOUR OFFSPRING'S INTELLIGENCE. (See **www.commercialfreechildhood.org**, the Campaign for a Commercial-Free Childhood's report on these items.) If you have bought them and listened to them with your baby, great. The baby has had the pleasure of your company. But the company has had the pleasure of your money.

Media as mentor? You bet
it is! How to shop, what to wear,
who to emulate, what's worth knowing.
The influence can be positive, neutral, or
counterproductive. If left to their own
resources to choose and interpret—what
THEY see is what WE'LL get.
Connie Thompson
TV News Anchor and Reporter

SPONGEHEADZ: U & MEdia

Tickle U is a programming line-up (or marketing ploy) from Cartoon Network. By assembling a menu of shows they think your baby will like, they have turned your household over to some very eager sponsors. The actual rationale used for this array was "to help develop your toddler's sense of humor."

"Children don't need TV to develop a sense of humor," said Wheelock College Professor Dr. Diane Levin, author of *Remote Control Childhood*. "This is a classic case of marketers trying to create a need where none exists and to dupe parents into thinking that watching more TV is good for their children."

Please—if your baby has to learn how to laugh from your TV, you've got far bigger problems at home than your choice of entertainment.

In fact, the issue that's most important is not what's on the air, but what's growing the kid from the inside out. We can start with breakfast.

Your toddler is already learning to identify products—just look at the juice aisle in your grocery store, with brightly colored *Sesame Street* character containers shelved at your child's eye level. This is only the beginning, folks.

In a recent NBC segment, kids as young as age two were able to identify corporate logos, not only on TV, but traveling in a car or bus. (The author's toddler would yell, "Madonna! Madonna!" He wasn't having a religious experience—he had just spotted the Golden Arches.)

Breakfast has some other problems, as well. Take Quaker Oats Instant Oatmeal—Strawberries and Cream, Peaches and Cream, or Blueberries and Cream.

The "blueberries" are dried figs dyed blue, with some blueberry concentrate. (Maybe. We're not sure.) Strawberries and Cream and Peaches and Cream are dehydrated apples dyed red and peach. And, as you might guess, according to CSPI, the Centers for Science in the Public Interest, the Quaker Instant Grits Country Bacon, Country Ham and Cheese, and Country Real Butter varieties have no bacon, ham, or butter. They do have textured protein, a cheese product, and something called "natural butter flavor." After one hundred years as a publicly traded company, Quaker Oats was bought by PepsiCo in 2001. Use this information to introduce to your kids the concept called "truth in advertising."

And then there's Popeye, the Sailor Man. The cartoon character, who hadn't flexed his muscles for some twenty years, recently became a "marketing partner" to King Features. According to the company's president, they are "positioning him for the next twenty-five years." Since 2004, he's appeared on Brawny Paper Towels, at NASCAR races, and has an iTunes deal with music maven Mark Mothersbaugh (*Rugrats* and many other shows for kids) to "reimagine" his signature song.

And you thought it was going to be about selling spinach! Well, River Ranch Spinach and Allen Canning Company are using Popeye on their packages and have made sure his mug gets a workout. He appears in mom-targeted media like *O, Good HouseKeeping*, and *Country Living*, as well as the women's Web site **www.iVillage.com**—and in all 161 Hearst newspapers (Hearst owns the magazines mentioned too.) DVDs, toys, games, in-park promotions at Universal Studios—Popeye is now a retro industry. For his seventy-fifth anniversary as a cartoon character, he was even linked to the National Council for Adoption when he "officially" adopted the baby Swee'pea. The move may have been well-intentioned, but the author and a lot of other adoptive parents found it exploitative and offensive.

It's just a theory, but perhaps King Features would be happy to see Popeye become the new SpongeBob Squarepants. As far as visibility and product tie-ins, TV's SpongeBob leaves Popeye way behind. Visit your grocery store and have your child count how many different times they can find SpongeBob's face.

Movie tie-ins are booming as well. *Star Wars: Episode III—Revenge of the Sith* plugged twenty-five different products, most of which had zero nutrients but an astronomical amount of calories. Cereals, snacks, fast food—"The movie sells the food, and the food sells the movie," said Susan Linn of CCFC. "It's a win-win for Lucas, FOX, and the food industries, but a losing proposition for families." Ditto *Cat in the Hat* and hundreds of other titles. Similar promotional campaigns are launched **every time there's a new "children's" film.**

Of course, commercials really hit pay dirt when they are launched from the small screen in the living room, especially when they masquerade as "counting books," from the makers of Skittles, Hershey's Chocolate, and M & M's.

Before we address the repeat offenders in the realm of food, let's start with you, the parent. You will read a great deal about how companies get you to SELECT their particular brands. But once the product gets home, how is it served?

One of the biggest ways parents can help prevent obesity is through PORTION CONTROL. We are encouraged to buy big meals and to serve dinner on big plates. The last thing parents need to do is to push kids into cleaning their plates if dinner has been high in fat, calories, sugar, or salt. So here's another Web site to check out: **www.theportionteller.com**. Lisa Young, Ph.D. and R.D. (registered dietician) created the site and wrote a book about easy ways to teach kids what an appropriate food portion actually is. You can help prevent a fat family future by visiting The Portion Teller. (Yes, add this to that book list.)

PAUSE

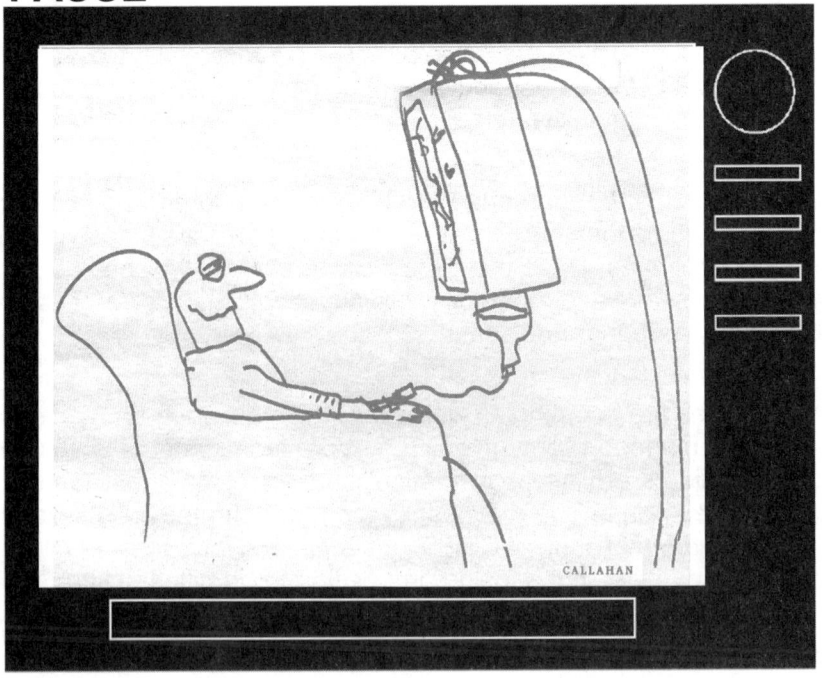

Lynn Ziegler

The biggest name in the fast-food frenzy is McDonald's. McDonald's, with its enclosed playgrounds, birthday parties, Happy Meals, toys, movie tie-ins, and Ronald the clown, has established a brand identity that even Wonder Woman couldn't shake if she tried. But McDonald's has learned a lot about media literacy lately.

Morgan Spurlock's 2005 *Super Size Me*, the documentary in which Spurlock chronicled thirty days of eating nothing but McDonald's food, was an eye opener to young and old alike. The negative effects on Spurlock's health were undeniable. Fortunately, he has since undone the damage by healthy eating, with an emphasis on fresh and locally grown foods, prepared by his wife, an organic chef.

In 2006, Eric Schlosser, the author of *Fast Food Nation*, and Charles Wilson, launched their new book, *Chew on This*, which explores the latest ways the fast-food industry contributes to poor health not just locally, but globally. Add this to the "I've gotta have this book" list for this chapter. Colorful, funny, and informative, it will teach something about fast food to every family member.

Still, McDonald's marches on. It has even investigated new kinds of commercials, pitched by Channel One, called "blinks." These commercials are **one second long**. They are designed to be used on radio, between songs and other spots. In case you were wondering, one second is just about long enough to sing "I'm Lovin' It." *Ad Age* calls this type of brand marketing "integrative, adaptive, and right in front of you," or in this case, whizzing by your ear. The TV blink has already been used in Belgium to sell breath mints that dissolve "in one second."

Then there's McDonald's hip-hop lyric campaign, and the announcement that McDonald's is sending its mascot to elementary schools to promote fitness and exercise. (And, perhaps, a new line of workout clothes.) Ronald's new title: "Chief Happiness Officer, the Ambassador for an active, balanced lifestyle." Although there have been some new additions to the menu, like "apple dippers" (in caramel) and "salad shakes" (with a very high-calorie dressing), the company still promotes the basic hit list: burgers, fries, and Chicken McNuggets.

Melinda Hemmelgarn, a Food and Society Policy Fellow with the Thomas Jefferson Agricultural Institute in Missouri, was decidedly underwhelmed by the news.

"Their goal in going into schools is, in a word, 'branding.' If Ronald was truly an ambassador of health, he would promote organic, sustainably produced foods, preferably from local producers, to support local economies and to protect the environment." Hemmelgarn, a nationally recognized nutritionist and advocate for kids' health, also addressed portion sizes as a key issue in kids' advertising.

You can check out her work at **www.foodsleuth@mschi.com**.

Susan Linn said, "McDonald's has no place in school," and agreed with Hemmelgarn that "the notion that kids need Ronald McDonald to get them to enjoy exercise is bogus. Given the opportunity, children naturally like to be active."

McDonald's has a kindergarten curriculum that "teaches children to 'Learn to Read Through Recognizing Corporate Logos." No kidding.

No doubt the legal team at McDonald's can't wait for the new documentary, *McLibel*, by Franny Armstrong. *McLibel* follows the trial of two Greenpeace activists who accused the corporation of exaggerating its food's nutritional value, exploiting children with its advertising, engaging in animal cruelty, underpaying its workers, and making food products that can cause heart disease. The trial began ten years after the two activists distributed leaflets that asked, "What's wrong with McDonald's?" Though they lost the original case and were ordered to pay fines of sixty thousand British pounds (reduced to forty thousand), and lost the first appeal, they filed a case against the United Kingdom in the European Court of Human Rights, and the court agreed with the activists. McDonald's says it has "moved on." *Their* appeal drags on.

But advertisers are wading into hotter water. Mega food conglomerate Kraft (owned by Altria, which used to be called Philip Morris and still sells cigarettes) has joined other major food companies and ad agencies to create a new lobbying group, The Alliance for American

Advertising, to *fight for the right to advertise to our kids*. The group's stated purpose is to "defend the industry's purported First Amendment rights to advertise to children, and to promote self-regulation, instead of having to submit to government regulation. General Mills is part of this movement, and why wouldn't it be? Between the two food giants, they spent $380 million on ads targeting kids in the United States *alone*.

CCFC gathered signatures supporting "A Statement on the Rights of Children, Families, and Food Marketers":

"It is alarming that, in the face of mounting evidence of harm associated with advertising to children, industry leaders are choosing to emphasize their rights without a commensurate focus on their responsibilities.

There is no absolute right to advertise to children.

Children, as both common sense and the law recognize, deserve special protections because of their developmental vulnerabilities."

Senator Tom Harkin (D-Iowa), who took the statement to Congress, is considered an ogre by the food industry. But he thinks Shrek—the cereal—is quite scary. He has been criticizing cereal companies for contributing to childhood obesity. Shrek cereal consists of sweetened corn puffs with marshmallow pieces, *and it contains fourteen grams of sugar in every serving.* "Kids just see that it's Shrek," Harkin says. See what a month of Shrekky breakfasts adds up to in terms of sugar intake: healthy eating advocates recommend taking a five-pound bag of sugar and actually measuring out a day's worth, a week's worth, and a month's worth of sugar from breakfast alone. Truly monstrous! And very scary, unless you are a dentist.

According to Dr. Linn, "Tie-ins are designed to lure children into selecting foods associated with their favorite movie or TV characters. They are also designed to *keep children continually reminded of products.* As one marketing expert says, corporations are "trying to establish a situation where kids are exposed to their brand in as many places as possible during the course of the day or week, or almost anywhere they turn in the course of their daily rituals."

Candy is seen as one of the few purchases kids make themselves, so marketers are encouraged to position "sweets" as a means of "fulfilling children's unmet needs for control."Author and ad guru Gene Del Vecchio reminds parents that kids have "very little control over their own lives—either at school, where the teacher is in charge, or at home, where parents set the ground rules." So candy choice becomes "empowerment."

But after the explosion of advertising that took place with expanded cable stations in the 1990s, children have become more of an influence on their parents' larger consumer purchases. One marketer told author Juliet Schor, "When I was growing up, (my) parents might say that I got to pick the color of the car. Now kids get to pick *the car*."

The food industry points out that it already has a self-regulatory watchdog group called the Children's Advertising Review Unit (CARU.) But nobody can find a single complaint filed by CARU with the Federal Trade Commission. Not one. Of course, when you consider that representatives of the food industries are its members, it's not that surprising. It sounds as successful as "government investigating itself."

Finally, a look at **advergames**. This kind of online advertising engages kids for long periods of time as they digitally "play" with their food. They can interact online with candy bars. They can watch Webisodes featuring Froot Loops' Toucan Sam and be charmed by Lucky the Leprechaun. Games are offered on 75 percent of the Web sites. More than 25 percent of the sites encourage kids to "join" so they can be told about new products and promotions. Fewer than half the sites require a parent's permission to do so. **Your child's personal information is mined at every site.**

The Kaiser Foundation released a report including these findings (and many more) in July 2006. The report, "It's Child's Play: Advergaming and the Online Marketing of Food to Children," analyzed seventy-seven Web sites and four thousand unique Web pages. *In a three-month period in 2005, these sites were visited by 12.2 million children, ages two to eleven.* Chances are that some of those kids were yours.

What can we do? We can steer our kids to Web sites like these:
www.commercialfreechildhood.org
www.pbs.org/dontbuyit/
www.nationaltelemediacouncil.org
www.action4mediaeducation.org
www.acmecoalition.org

The last two groups offer two different educational packets for families and teachers each called "Food For Thought."

We can get our families to make healthier choices, drink water instead of pop, and cut down if not eliminate altogether, patronage of fast-food establishments. We can point out the flaws in commercials and discourage kids from "playing with their food" online. Media literacy education teaches kids and parents to be healthy skeptics, rather than cynics.

> **Children's health *and* our democracy depend on critical thinking and active citizenship. We need to make watching TV (and food commercials) a participatory sport.**
> Melinda Hemmelgarn, a.k.a.
> "The Food Sleuth"

Thanks to Susan Linn, Ph.D. for material from *Consuming Kids: Protecting Our Kids From the Onslaught of Marketing and Advertising*, throughout the SELECT section.

And we can quote—daily—a certain "food film's" best line:

> **Never eat food that's served
> by tossing it out of a window—unless
> you're a seagull.**
> Morgan Spurlock, Documentarian and Producer
> *Super Size Me*

STUFF WE THINK WE NEED

Let's take a look at how we become convinced that we need more "stuff" in the first place. George Carlin, where are you when we need you? (Carlin's riff on "What to do with our 'stuff'" should be required listening/viewing for anyone with credit cards or cash. In other words, all of us.)

Marketing is as old as trade itself, and its sneakiest ally lives at your house.

Nothing works quite as well as nagging. In fact, "pester power" is something marketers count on to get you into the store to make that SELECTion.

In a media release for Western Media International (now called Initiative Media Worldwide) titled *The Fine Art of Whining: Why Nagging Is a Kid's Best Friend,* we learn how confident advertisers are in that concept.

Who gives in? In order: divorced parents; parents with teenagers or babies; and the most vulnerable, the "combos" of the two.

What is nagged for?

Four out of ten kids nag to go to entertainment or food venues, such as Discovery Zone or Chuck E. Cheese's

Three in ten nag for videos and DVDs

One in three nags for a trip to a fast food restaurant. Five minutes ago.

Nagging accounts for 46 percent of sales in key businesses that target children. This is a science. There are three basic types of nagging:

Persistence Nagging: the request is repeated again and again and again.

Importance Nagging: a modified guilt trip ("I need the Barbie Dream House so that Ken and Barbie can live together and have children and have their own family." Actual quote.)

Subversive Nagging: "I'll just ask Grandma" or new stepdad or the other parent.

The *Selling to Kids Newsletter* described a research project in which 150 mothers with children ranging in age from three to eight were asked to keep track of "requests" (read: a "nagging diary") for two weeks.

The Nag Factor reported, collectively, ten-thousand nags. That breaks down to sixty-six per mom, or 4.7 per day over the two weeks. That number increases with children aged nine and above, with the "magic number" (the point at which the parent caves in) at nine, seventeen, or thirty-one, depending on which study you use. Nagging peaks in early adolescence at around fifty nags a day.

Parents are divided into three types:

The Indulgers: There is another word for them: PUSHOVERS. These parents always give in. They just want to have fun, to be their kids' pals, and play with the new remote control car or video game. Frequently, the spouse of an Indulger refers to him (rarely a her) as "my other child."

The Conflicted: These are single or divorced parents whose purchasing choices are often influenced by guilt. ("Don't worry, Mom, I can just ask _____ for it.") The Conflicted are easy prey for a subversive nagger.

The Pragmaparents: These good folks can live with what their children consider "bare necessities" (the basics, not the lingerie store) of life. They are practical and thrifty and can fend off even the worst, most persistent naggers. Sounds like you, right?

But they are up against, as we all are, billions of dollars, not just in the messages and their production, but in the money paid to experts to break down our barriers, and the legal teams to represent the companies who eventually are taken to task for misrepresentation and outright malfeasance.

It's monstrous materialism, and here is a gallery of scenes to remember.

"Product placement" used to be just a shameless plug in a movie, easily accomplished by having the label on a bag of chips face the camera, announcing to the audience, "Dude—Keanu Reeves (of *Bill and Ted's Excellent Adventure*) is eating Doritos, just like you!" Well, that was then—this is now.

Product placement is now so much a part of nightly TV programming that it may not even be consciously registering with you anymore.

Look at *Extreme Makeover: Home Edition*. Sears paid $1 million for the first season for commercials PLUS verbal and visual references to its products *in every episode*. "This also explains those lingering camera shots of folks weeping for joy over Kenmore washing machines," writes Beth Gillin in *The Inquirer. American Idol was* paid a similar sum by Coke.

If you've noticed a lot of new labels on old, familiar products, there's a good reason: Many corporations, like Cold Stone Creamery, are *redesigning their packaging so that it will stand out better on-screen.* ***ANY screen!***

Packaging has been contributing to not only obesity, but environmental waste. Now it has even spawned a new behavior, called "wrap rage"—sixty-thousand documented cases of people actually injuring themselves while struggling to open molded plastic packaging. (Admit it: you've had the same problem after a trip to a hardware store or a toy store, which really are not all that different.)

In product placement, the item doesn't even have to be visible any more—it can be mentioned in the scripts of any show. Jerry Seinfeld's occasional references to Thin Mints have been totally eclipsed by dialogue that drops sponsor names several times a segment. And, of course, between segments, there are more commercials!

Writers for shows carried by major networks have asked the Writers Guild to put a halt to this practice. Other show business unions are joining the writers because some of their members say, "It's 'stealth advertising.' It deceives the audiences, and it forces writers and actors to do jobs they were not hired for."

"We are being told to write the lines that sell this merchandise, and to disguise this sale as 'story,'" said one writer.

In one reality show episode, an argument broke out between cast members. Part of a scene had to be reshot—not because of the argument, but **because one of the contestants had accidentally covered the brand on the can of soda.** Think about the material in the button/chapter "EDIT." The scene—showing only the hands—was redone, and the editors fixed the problem, while still keeping the argumentative audio. The fight stayed intact, with a few cuts here and there, and so did the agreement with the soda company.

Contestants on *The Apprentice* were asked to write a new jingle for Burger King. American Express was specifically mentioned in dialogue numerous times in *The Restaurant*.

These hardly seem to earn the designation of "reality" show.

But other programs are dealing with even more subtle issues.

SPONGEHEADZ: U & MEdia

Free speech advocates have been concerned about the fact that media consolidation (when only a few companies control most of the media) has led to situations where content is bent to corporate or governmental will. For example, since the Carter and Reagan administrations, the White House Office of National Drug Control Policy actually reviews the messages incorporated in television scripts.

buy me
Stuff for
crismass Ezra

Under the guise of the Family Friendly Programming Forum, big advertisers, such as Coca-Cola, McDonald's, Kelloggs, and General Mills, gave money toward the development of "family friendly" shows— ones that would be free of violence and sexual content. One of their best creations is a really positive show, *Gilmore Girls*. It was sponsored by Kelloggs. "Guess what the Gilmore Girls ate for breakfast?" asks Susan Linn in *Consuming Kids*. "Kelloggs' Pop Tarts." She adds, "Given the childhood obesity epidemic, just how family-friendly are the advertising practices of food companies like Kellogg's, General Mills, Coca-Cola, and McDonald's? Is any corporation in the business of marketing to children truly family-friendly?"

And it gets worse. "The Forum offers scriptwriting scholarships to film school at NYU and USC. It has provided seed money to some networks to create programming. Will a beneficiary of one of these scholarships be likely to write a show that's critical of, say, the advertising industry? How much influence will a Forum scholarship have on the creativity of cash-strapped film students?" asks Linn.

Inquiring, media-savvy spongeheadz want to know.

If you remember Hot Wheels, those little racing cars, get ready to reimagine them as they are pitched to a new generation. The new ad campaign will not just be pictures in a Toys "B" Mine catalog; there will be "a multi-faceted series of entertainment-based toy promotions, including animated and live-action feature films," according to Ad Age's Web site, **www.madisonandvine.com** ("where Commerce meets Content"). That says it all.

British parents don't like what's happening any more than we do, as they buy a lot of American products. They're dealing with "advergaming," too.

"When children read books or play games, they are at their most receptive to learning and suggestion," said Kath Dalmeny, author of a new report to the food commission. Her work cites the Frosties TigerCathlon Web site, where children can earn points by taking part in races in a virtual stadium, but only if their cartoon characters pick up packets of Frosties to give them enough "power."

Kelloggs, who manufactures Frosties (the British version of Tony the Tiger's Frosted Flakes) used the phrase "train hard, eat right, and earn your stripes" to try to convince children that its products were healthy. But the study criticized the slogan, noting that a thirty gram bowl of Frosties had more sugar than "a jam doughnut, a custard tart, or a flapjack (pancake)."

Coke, in particular, has been singled out by children's organizations for targeting children with in-school advertising, product placement, toys, and contests—promoting a product that has no nutritional value. Coke was recently dropped by a major investment fund, TIAA-CREF, for marketing "nutritionally **deficient** products to children" as well as for concerns about "widespread labor, human rights, and environmental abuses," according to a CCFC media release. MTV's animated show, *Daria*, created a brilliant send-up of this problem in an episode called "Fizz." In it, a cash-strapped school enters into an agreement with a soda company to get a new, $50,000 electronic scoreboard for the football team. When the school fails to meet its sales quota, teachers are provided "learning aids" (a solar-system mobile consisting of cans of the product). Eventually the cheerleading squad is forced to wear uniforms designed to look like the soda cans. Daria, one of the smartest animated characters on TV, finally convinces the school superintendent to visit the logo-covered walls of the high school, and he arrives just in time to watch the principal in extreme melt-down, being carried off to a place where she could get some "rest." And a lot of meds.

Jean Kilbourne is the author of *Can't Buy My Love: How Advertising Changes the Way We Think and Feel,* and *Deadly Persuasion: Why Women and Girls Must Fight the Addictive Power of Advertising.* Her award-winning documentaries on how sexuality is marketed (to our daughters especially) are powerful indictments of industry exploita-tion of girls. *Killing Us Softly, Slim Hopes,* and *Calling the Shots* are three of the reasons that *The New York Times Magazine* acknowl-edged her as one of the three most popular speakers on college cam-puses today. She has made a career of watching how marketing zeroes in on the female gender.

She quotes Cartoon Network as saying, "Today's kids influence over $130 billion of their parents' spending annually. That makes these little consumers **big business**." She adds that the president of Kids "R" Us says, "If you own this child at an early age, you can own this child for years to come." Companies are saying, "Hey, I want to own this kid younger and younger." This is why brand identification is so important to the corporations targeting our kids.

Jean Kilbourne was scheduled to appear on a segment of *The Today Show* in 2005 to talk about this very subject. But at the last minute, she was cancelled because the producers decided to do an interview on…new products and how they were about to be marketed. (This segment has been brought to you by the Department of Irony. AUTHOR'S NOTE: I couldn't make this up if I tried.) Kilbourne finally appeared on *The Today Show* in August 2006.

Shortly after the movie *Finding Nemo* was released, Shell gas came out with a new commercial that mimicked scenes from the film, in which "commuter" fish joined many others in a huge current, en route to work. The spot ran for almost two years in many markets. Did it appeal to parents who actually drove their kids to see the film? Not exactly, although it was cute. But ten years from now, **when that child is driving**, will they remember the Shell sign at the bottom of the sea and be favorably disposed to pull in and gas up? You betcha.

Kilbourne quotes respected researcher George Gerbner as saying, "For the first time in human history, most of the stories about people, life, and values are told not by parents, schools, churches, or others in the community who have something to tell, **but by a group of distant conglomerates that have something to sell**." Kilbourne says,"The stories that most influence our children these days are the stories told by **advertisers**."

Some people say that it's time for commercials to go. It may sound radical, but consider the fact that many children, especially young ones, can't differentiate between a show and its advertisers.

And from 1991-2003, time given to commercials and other promotional messages increased by 36 percent. In a three-hour block of prime time, from 8 to 11 p.m., each of the four networks offers fifty-two minutes of advertising. You might be watching TV for three hours, but almost one hour of that was commercials *only*.

Can you imagine TV without commercials? Probably not. But perhaps it's time to try.

Can you imagine TV without commercials that target children? That's what the European Union (EU) is considering—no commercials targeting anyone under thirteen. It's already being done in some Scandinavian countries—yes, the ones with higher literacy rates and less rampant materialism than ours.

EVERYTHING ELSE

There is one commodity that is marketed to us endlessly:

FEAR

Think about it. Fear is the ploy that moves products. Fear of being overweight. Fear of hair loss or financial loss. Fear of aging ("How do you like being older? Well, *that DEPENDS*," is how baby boomers are being pitched the hazards of middle age.) Viagra? Breath mints? Investments? Plastic surgery? Hummers? *Fear Factor* isn't just a show anymore, it's a way of life.

There are entire industries built around our fears, but the biggest one is the one our tax dollars are supporting: our own government. Whether it's privatizing Social Security, The USA PATRIOT Act, or the latest episode in the color-coded Global War on Terror, we are being bombarded by messages confirming how scared we are supposed to be.

TV messages that promote fear need to be identified and deconstructed. When you recognize that someone is trying to sell you fear, you are working to take it out of the equations of daily life. FEAR is going to be a strategic choice in marketing candidates in the run-up to the next two elections. The only way to inoculate yourself against this pixel-pocked, digital disease is media literacy.

FEAR is not a healthy atmosphere for children.

Air America talk show host Randi Rhodes puts it this way:

FEAR:
DON'T BUY ANY!

The point of media literacy is to create SMART MEDIA CONSUMERS. So....

ZAP

1. Run, do not walk, to your nearest library and take out the HBO trilogy, sponsored by *Zillions Magazine* (the kid-version of *Consumer Reports*) called *Buy Me That!, Buy Me That, Too!,* and *Buy Me That III.* The trio provides an eye-opening look at how TV commercials are made. Among the highlights: learning about Food Fashionistas (OK, they are called "dressers" for a reason. Watching a hamburger as it is "dressed for success" by a professional television artist is a lesson you'll remember for years—especially the next time you watch a fast food commercial.) Yes, some of the commercials are from the 1980s, but the ideas are still being used every day.

2. Starvation and famine are not limited to the African continent.

   Open your children's eyes some evening by offering to serve them a typical sub-Saharan dinner: a little bit of rice, or flour, perhaps with a mashed vegetable. Maybe. If they're lucky.

   Then help your kids start a food drive to restock a local food bank. You can approach the manager of a local movie theater a few weeks before the opening of a blockbuster movie (A Harry Potter film works great, because you can invite participants to "make magic happen.") Pixar flicks work too! Organize your plan around Saturday afternoon matinees, preferably during a rainy month. Many theaters are willing to give discount coupons for popcorn if two nonperishable items are donated by each child.

   Warning: This campaign works a lot like the multiplying broom scene from *The Sorcerer's Apprentice.* Once the theater opens, you may need to arrange for caravans of trucks to take the food where it's needed most! (A Saturday's worth of magic—three showings in two theatres—stocked three western Washington food banks.) Make sure you have a donation jar for people who didn't know about the food drive, but who want to make an on-the-spot donation. The three

food banks in question not only got tons of food (literally) but several hundred dollars apiece.

3. Read *Chew on This.* Warning: When the author's youngest read *Fast Food Nation* as part of an eighth grade project, he became a vegetarian. Suggestion: If you haven't done so already, cheerfully embrace soy products. If they are Amazon-grown (killing the rainforest to save herds of cattle is counterproductive at best), lobby against the soybean conglomerates and find other sources for healthier, "happier" meals. Thankfully, as we go to print, McDonald's has chosen a different soybean market source, and other fast-food giants will hopefully follow Ronald's lead.)

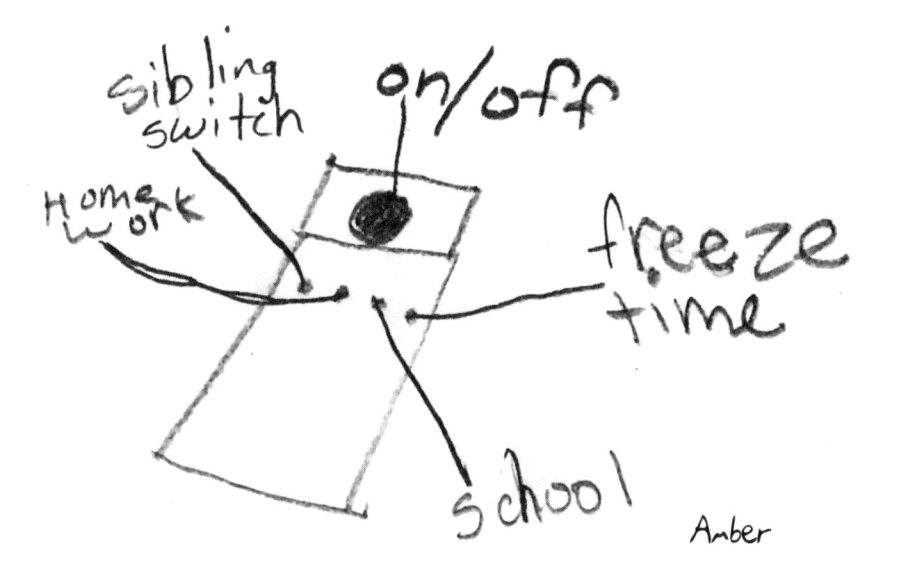

VOLUME (OF) VIOLENCE

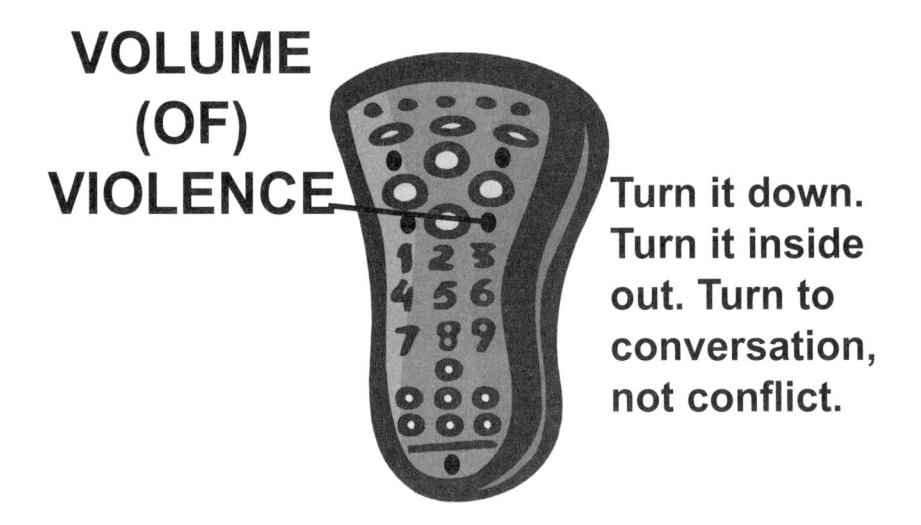

Turn it down. Turn it inside out. Turn to conversation, not conflict.

Ask any parent what's wrong with TV, and the V-word comes up. Not the V-chip, which is a possible solution, but the V-word: violence.

Two things frighten kids more than anything else: One is fear of abandonment; the other is fear of being physically hurt.

That pretty much covers the scare-driven plot lines of not only a great deal of television programming, but the movies that will end up on your TV (in edited form). And a lot of the news of the past two years.

With that in mind, consider what the Katrina coverage and the tsunami stories did to the children who survived them, as well as the kids who tuned in and saw the carnage.

Ten months after Katrina,
its emotional effect on children is
proving to be long and lasting. Two
studies of (Katrina) children affected by the
hurricane found high rates of depression,
anxiety, behavioral problems, and even post-
traumatic stress disorder.
Julia Cass, *Washington Post* 6.13.06

The numbers tell the story.

According to Cass's article, Louisiana State University mental health screening of nearly five thousand children in schools and temporary housing in the state found that:

- 96 percent saw hurricane damage to their own homes or neighborhoods
- 22 percent had relatives and friends who were injured
- 14 percent had relatives and friends who died
- 35 percent lost their pets
- 34 percent were separated from their primary caregivers at some point during the disaster—and 9 percent still are.

"The concern for the Katrina children is not just the immediate trauma from the storm, but that so much of their lives remains disrupted," she observed.

Kids in New Orleans frequently check *The Weather Channel* nearly a year after the disasters. One eight-year-old girl, according to Cass, is convinced that the next storm will be a "category eight"—a designation that doesn't exist—yet.

According to a 2005 BBC study of kids aged nine to thirteen, children find television images of violent news events *more disturbing than fictional violence, and can distinguish clearly between the two.* (Younger children, of course, are mightily disturbed by both.)

The study suggests that images of real violence have the greater effect, especially if they affect **other children or people and places with which they identify.** Violence pictured in a familiar environment, or a place children considered secure, was seen as more threatening than violence in a fantasy landscape. So a twisted clown in a neighborhood park, like Stephen King's murderous Pennywise in *It* (which produced an entire generation of kids terrified by clowns!) is a whole lot creepier than, say, the over-the-top *Killer Clowns from Outer Space.* As usual, it is the breakdown of the familiar that terrifies our children.

Unsurprisingly, the same survey found that boys were far more likely to have sought out and seen images of violence than girls, and that boys in particular enjoyed special effects (SFX) producing blood, guts, and gore, *especially if they did not feel threatened.*

A simple SFX lesson can be done in your kitchen: any kid with access to chocolate syrup can become a dripping, menacing vampire in about thirty seconds. (Chocolate syrup photographs like blood.) In fact, the mother of SFX Wizard Rick Baker, who worked on *Star Wars, Harry and the Hendersons, Men in Black I & II,* The Ring I & II, and more, used to come home from work to find her ten-year-old on the kitchen floor, sporting a variety of gory wounds he'd created with stuff from the refrigerator. (He also used flour to create and bake his own fake prostheses, scabs, scars, and claws.) Eventually the shock value wore off, and Mrs. Baker would simply step over the "body" and start dinner. Thirty-five movies and forty years later, the Oscars her son collects (six and counting!) have nothing to do with hot dogs.

> **Mom, did you see that last scene? They must've used a *gallon* of the stuff!**
> Chris Crockett, age 10, in his living room, contemplating his future in the horror genre

But fantasy violence is one thing, and real violence is quite another.

Besides, violence is a moneymaker.

According to *Gun Play and Greed: The Marketing of Violence to Children,* by Nancy Carlsson-Paige, Ed.D., selling violence to kids began in the Reagan administration in 1984, when the FCC deregulated the broadcasting industry. Suddenly, it was legal to use TV to market toys and other products to children. TV and toymakers hooked up to market toy-linked shows, and a year later, ***all of the top ten toys, most of them violent, were linked to television.***

And it's not just the link between TV and toys that is problematic. Now, it's a cross-platform, full-blown assault on children, with Hollywood movies, videos, computer games, foods, books, fast-food tie-ins, and the Internet targeting the people least prepared for such an attack.

The Canadian Media Awareness Network (**www.mediaawareness. ca./english/resources**) has an excellent report on television violence that echoes the findings of similar work in the United States and the United Kingdom. "At ages six to eleven, the kids develop a surprising taste for horror movies, perhaps deliberately scaring themselves in an attempt to overcome their own fears."

But what do kids think violence is?

Generally, kids understand violence as the intent to do harm. Violence can be physical (punching, kicking, shooting) and it can be verbal (ridicule, insults, and put-downs.) It can be psychological, as demonstrated by the "two greatest fears" mentioned earlier in this section.

One kind of violence appears as a recurrent theme in kids' TV, and it is among the most lethal. We need to remember the lessons of Columbine, Colorado, and Red Lake, Minnesota.

You can predict long-term havoc when a child is bullied.

Technology has given us a new twist on that old probem: cyber-bullying. The folks at the Seattle-based Committee for Children (**www. cfchildren.org**) have developed extensive resources to assist parents in dealing with this latest wrinkle in harassment.

"Cyber-bullies" are using high-tech methods to tease, taunt, and intimidate other students. The weapons are e-mail, instant messaging, Wi-Fi-connected laptops, cell phones, text messages and Web site creation. The victims find themselves attacked by embarrassing images, negative comments, threats, and profanity that are then e-mailed to large groups of students for what can only be described as "humilitainment."

It's using the "third screen" itself to hurt another child, and parents need to know how to deal with both the victim and the perpetrator.

Cyber-bullying causes pain just as real as traditional bullying and is in some ways more frightening, since the victim is chased into his or her own home and can still be surrounded by it. You can turn off the cell phone, but eventually it will ring again.

So, the experts at CCF and Children Now suggest that parents remember to teach kids that if they have personal issues with another student, they should express them. Parents need to emphasize that it is NOT OK to say anonymously what they are unable to say to another kid's face. Expressing hate messages anonymously (and to hundreds of people at a time, at the victim's expense) is wrong, wrong, wrong.

Don't deny your child Internet access. That won't solve the problem, and it may deny your kid the chance to do homework. It's essentially punishing the victim. You can find out the source. The upside of technology is that these kinds of attacks are traceable in many cases. **Middle school students, who are the prime age range for this activity, should be aware that there are legal penalties for committing an electronic assault on another child.** This situation is becoming so prevalent that you can expect to see this storyline woven into programming for young adults in the very near future.

Video games, according to Carlsson-Paige, are replacing more creative and socially interactive forms of play after school. But many of these games are violent, and once they are in the home, younger kids will play them, too.

"Everywhere they turn, children are bombarded with messages about violence that undermine the lessons parents are trying to teach," she wrote.

What's needed? Carlsson-Paige recommends the following:

Public education—media literacy—for parents, so they can better understand how entertainment violence can harm our kids. Some patterns of aggressive behavior at age eight are highly predictive of aggressive behavior in adulthood.) Remember, our children absorb everything.

An FCC that actively protects children from entertainment violence.

Creation of an independent ratings board, one that operates outside of industry control, to provide age-based ratings for TV programs, movies, video games, and toys. (AUTHOR'S NOTE: The current TV ratings system doesn't address content issues adequately.)

An FTC that regulates marketing of violence to children, especially the youngest audience members.

The Center for Media Literacy has published a handout, *The Six Myths of Media Violence*, to help parents combat the often-repeated statement that "nothing can be done to challenge or reduce media violence." (The author has added some material to these categories.)

Myth #1: I saw lots of violence when I was a kid and I turned out OK.

But when a child becomes an adult, s/he may become a victim of the **fear** of violence, so distrustful of others that s/he will turn his or her back on a friend in need, rather than risk being harmed. Mass-media storytelling reinforces the myths, beliefs, and attitudes of a culture of violence. The issue is not just whether an individual turns out OK, but whether *society* turns out OK.

Myth #2: Media violence simply reflects what is going on in real life.

Research shows that sensationalized coverage of murders, rapes, and disasters is far out of proportion to their frequency in real life (although the author takes issue with that last one.) Frequent violence sends kids a message that violent behavior is an easy and acceptable way to express anger and resolve conflict.

Myth #3: Violence is a natural part of drama. Some argue that watching violence can actually REDUCE anger and violent impulses in certain individuals.

There is a big difference between seeing dead bodies onstage in Hamlet (who could have used a line from *The Sixth Sense:* "I see dead people") and spending hours on end "wasting the enemy" in a violent video game. Catharsis in drama is the resolution of human conflict—eventually, the main character can regret his terrible acts. **But action-adventure entertainment makes violence an end in itself.** Those who use violence are not humans who feel remorse—they become killing machines, characters portrayed as somewhat heroic *because* they are violent. (Yes, little Terminators.)

Myth #4: Decisions about viewing media violence should be left up to parents.

Parents need to develop new skills to deal with the barrage of media messages faced by our kids. And kids need to be educated to critically evaluate those messages. It really does take a village to raise a child, and in the electronic village that's even more true. We are all responsible for the cultural environment of our kids. Media makers and media owners need to be held accountable when what is meant to pass as entertainment contributes to the deterioration of empathy and the desensitization that comes with a diet of media violence.

Myth #5: We live in a country that constitutionally protects free speech. I don't like violence, but I don't want censorship.

Learn some discretion. When public opinion makes gratuitous violence unacceptable as entertainment, change can happen. (AUTHOR'S NOTE: Censorship is not an option. Education

is! Parents can even use examples of on-screen violence to teach nonviolence.)

Myth #6: Violence is what people want to see. If people don't want to see it, they can turn off the TV or not spend money on violent videos, games, or movies.

Some kids watch seven to eight hours of TV a day, and may continue to do so throughout their lives. It begins in childhood, but violence in entertainment is used as a marketing strategy to reach that prime demographic—eighteen- to forty-nine-year-old males who have money to spend on whatever the sponsors of the show are selling. (The strategy for selling to girls and women is quite different.) Adrenalin and testosterone are a profitable blend, and changing that mix is going to be challenging. Violence—in media and real life—is America's most visible export. If we want our children to see a more positive world, we need to balance their media intake.

To that end, there is a ray of light on the usually dark and dangerous world of video games, and the arrival of these socio-political strategy games could not be more timely. One game is called *Peacemaker*, in

which there is real-world immersion and real-time crisis, based on the Israeli-Palestinian conflict. This game, and other persuasive strategy games like it, can be used as a medium for change, because games can illustrate complex situations. Developers of these games include the MacArthur Foundation and other well-known philanthropic organizations. One game is based on providing humanitarian aid through the United Nations, and includes having to deal with warlords and corruption. Another "persuasive" game features scenarios in which the players need to escape from mercenaries while searching for water. 700,000 people played it the first month it became available, free, and of those, **tens of thousands entered the "political action" area of the game and sent e-mails to politicians demanding assistance for the people of Darfur.**

Admittedly, not everyone will choose this kind of entertainment, no matter how terrific the graphics are. But isn't it good to know that there's a positive alternative to *Grand Theft Auto: San Andreas*?

Check out some of the statistics on TV violence in the button marked **NUMB3RS**. And explore the resources of the many organizations currently addressing this issue.

Counting the numbers of body blows and injuries is not a plan.

There are people who accumulate (and quote) those statistics, but still expose kids to violent programming, rationalizing their lack of supervisory skills with the "Six Myths," or worse, letting a child watch a violent show because it's inconvenient to change the channel.

What a child learns about violence, a child learns for life.
Cable PSA on reducing domestic violence

Let the technology work for you, not against you. V-chips and parental "locks" have become more user-friendly. (However, you may have to create an unusual code so that your child doesn't figure out how to unlock the device and regain access to violent programming.) Cable networks, which are not yet bound by the same restrictions as broadcast channels, have launched a series of PSAs encouraging parents to "take (remote) control" in a hands-on way. Given the current state of globally broadcast violent images, including some that happen live, on-air, this is smart advice.

So, if you take only one idea from this chapter, make it this one:

The most important reason to work to reduce media violence is that repeatedly viewing it desensitizes children in a way that makes them less likely to respond _when someone in real life is in trouble_.

The solution to dealing with violent programming is to develop enough empathy and compassion in your child that viewing violence is something _they_ actively choose not to do.

1. Ask your child if s/he knows what the term "domestic violence" means, and if s/he knows anyone it happens to.

   Hitting is not the only form it takes—verbal abuse can have effects that are just as lasting. If you suspect a child is being abused, cyber-wise or otherwise, ACT—through a counselor, a school professional, an agency, or a relative. In an era in which violence to kids abounds, it's better to be able to make an apology than make a trip to a courtroom— or a memorial service.

2. We can (AND MUST!) get our kids to consider nonviolence in our daily lives _first_. Encourage your child to act on the belief that conversation trumps physical confrontation. But preparedness is important, too—remind your child that no

one should stand by while someone is being hurt. Role-play. Have a "kid-code" if your child is being picked up at school or an activity by someone other than yourself. Make sure your kids always know whom to call if you're not available, and that they know their address. Alert them to stranger danger, but make sure they know that there are always good adults around to help—first responders, firefighters, police, teachers, and others—so that they feel empowered.

3. The term "nonviolent conflict resolution" describes how most episodes of stories in a distant future are resolved; *Star Trek: Next Generation* is an example. Rent, record, or download some old episodes. Then start suggesting ALTERNATIVE NONVIOLENT SOLUTIONS to the endings of other shows. After that, you can move on to real-life events on the news.

Explain in the simplest terms why one group is fighting another, and see what your kids come up with as a fair solution.

Be sure to share all sides of the conflict.

Then send your family's solutions to current global crises to your Congressional representatives.

It can only help.

All we are saying is
'Give peace a chance.'
John Lennon

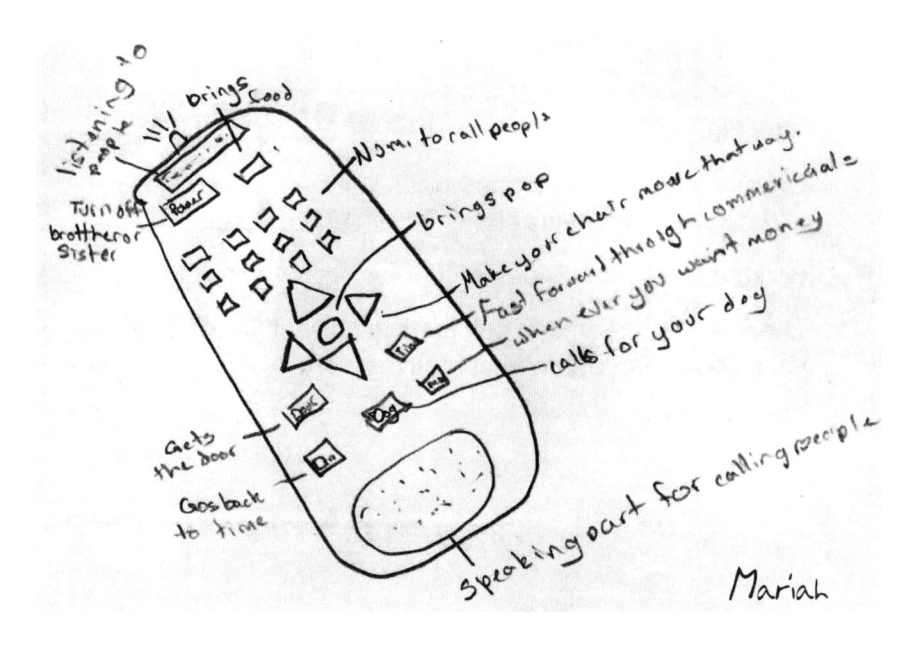

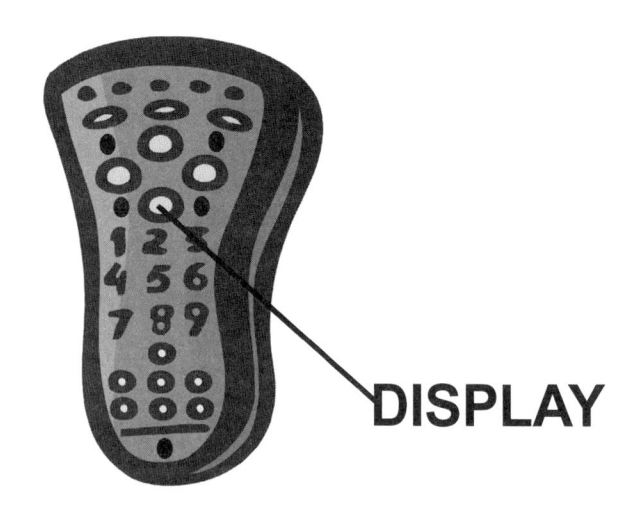

DISPLAY

This button will demand a great deal of news time in the next few years. The issue of what's "on display" on our TV screens is a prism. Our core beliefs color our tolerance—or lack thereof.

How we handle or react to what's on display depends on cultural influences like religion, politics, individual upbringing, and what is or isn't "age appropriate."

Coming to terms with family limits of what's on display *should not be done while you're watching the show in question.* Familiarize yourself with the programming first. **Whatever you decide, be consistent.**

Some questions to ask your family include the following:

Just what are those people doing? What's the best way to handle passion or extraordinarily graphic violence when it suddenly appears in front of us in the living room? When is nudity OK? What about body parts? Where do you draw the line at public displays of affection? Are your boundaries reflective of racial, ethnic, or lifestyle concerns? How graphic is the violence you and your kids choose to watch? (And remember—that *is* a choice.)

Also, it's not just about what you see, but what you hear.

Going "live" is becoming more hazardous than ever.

This year (2006) the FCC has asked broadcasters for tapes that include vulgar remarks uttered at live sporting events by players, coaches, and even unruly spectators. As this book goes to print, two of the areas under scrutiny are football games and NASCAR events.

Russell Shaw, writing for *ZDNet*, offers this example:

"Like, say, a group of partisan fans, out in the cheap seats, utters a barnyard expletive when they felt that the football receiver, called out of bounds at the back of the end zone, had both feet in bounds and should have been credited with a touchdown......the fine: as much as $325,000 for each instance."

Keep in mind that on July 17, 2006, the President of the United States used the same "barnyard expletive" near an open microphone during a lunch photo-op at the G8 Summit in a conversation with British Prime Minister Tony Blair. As the conflict between the Israelis and Hezbollah and Hamas continued to escalate over the kidnapping of an Israeli soldier, the President (with a mouthful of food, no less!) said to Blair, on camera and audio-tape:

"The irony is, what they need to do is get Syria to get Hezbollah to stop doing this shit, and it's over." (CNN)

CNN ran the comment unfiltered, since cable stations are not (yet) bound by the Broadcast Decency Enforcement Act of 2006. But the networks bleeped out the expletive to avoid the fine. If the law is changed to cover cable networks, would they be fined just once, or for every time the clip aired? The blogosphere had a field day, with many writers suggesting that the President ante up and be the first to pay the penalty.

The FCC in 2006 is split three to two in favor of the President's party, but has had to deal with open mic problems before—as has every administration.

However, with electronics owned by so many members of the public (not just news-gathering organizations), reporting of these incidents seems to be increasing. In a rather ignominious first, on the Senate floor, Vice President Dick Cheney told Senator Leahy to perform a physically impossible sex act upon himself. And that word—the dreaded "F-word" (or "F-bomb," as it is called in some circles) presents an even bigger problem. The F-word, in its adverbial/adjectival form, was used by a surprised rocker, Bono, when he won a prestigious music award at a live show. At first, the FCC ruled that, because he was not using the F-word in its literal sense (a crude word for a sexual act), the stations airing the show would not be fined.

Then came the Super Bowl episode that changed everything. Janet Jackson's "wardrobe malfunction" (at the hand of Justin Timberlake) resulted in provisions by the FCC that raised the previous fines of $32,000 for "indecency" **ten times over**. The inspiration for the BDEA had arrived.

PAUSE

Networks, not wanting to face the new, stiffer penalties, began editing (or declining to run) shows that could get very costly in two seconds or two syllables. There was a huge confab over whether or not the film *Saving Private Ryan* could be run on Veteran's Day with its language intact (including the military's frequent use of the offending verb.) A network chose to cancel an episode of an award-winning, late prime-time medical program that *partially* showed a woman's breast as she was undergoing a health exam. Fear of the fine became contagious.

Contrast this with the fact that far bigger "sins"—like a large cable company's depriving a small rural community of VoIP services (voice-operated Internet protocols). The fine? Fifteen thousand dollars.

Think about this, and walk through it again, won't you? The FCC fine for blocking VoIP and depriving less-affluent people in rural America access to twenty-first century technology? Fifteen thousand dollars.

The FCC fine for airing a chant from a drunken crowd? Three hundred twenty-five thousand dollars.

What's wrong with this picture (or MP3 file)?

As incomprehensible as this may seem, it led to the following Internet headline:

To FCC, Crowd-Cussing is 21.67 Times as Bad as Net Neutrality Violations

Russell Shaw ends his piece with the following observation: "…in the bizarre world where deliberate, net-neutrality subverting technical malfunctions are OK, but wardrobe malfunctions (a la Justin and Janet) are a mortal sin, nanoseconds of boobs flash and cussing is *21.67 times more of a sin against the public good than subverting competing Internet services*." (Italics and bold font by author of this book.)

If you can claim never to have used the words in question, good for you.

The author cannot make that claim, and neither can most of the people she knows. But a visit to any schoolyard will surprise you with the depth of vocabulary your children may be exposed to (and are, perhaps, using themselves, without your knowledge) every day. This does not mean that you should give up the fight to expand your child's vocabulary (and perhaps your own) by finding other words to express anger, frustration, and, in Bono's case, great joy. No one is going to establish "the soap in the mouth" police force any time soon, much to the disappointment of some parents, grandparents, and caregivers. But all of us can establish limits and make an effort to stick to them.

ZAP

1. Decide what your family's comfort zone is in the areas of language, visuals, fantasy violence—and the real thing. Discuss violence in animation, and see if your kids think a scene is less violent if it looks like a comic book.

2. Discuss your particular family guidelines with your family. Do the TV ratings systems apply in your house? Do you know how to "block" certain programs? Does **M** stand for "Mature" or "Mommmmm, my friends' parents let *them* watch it"?

3. How does your family deal with inappropriate language?

   What happens if, in a live event, someone says or does something that needs to be bleeped out? Is there a disconnect between the language your kids hear at school, and the words you don't want heard in your living room? Talk about this with your family. Fearlessly!

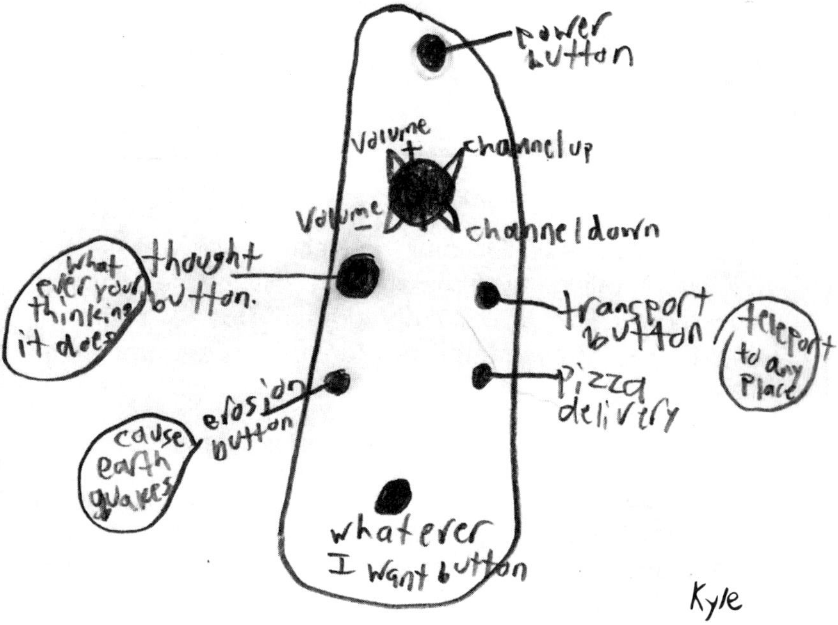

138

SPONGEHEADZ: U & MEdia

power button

Volume + channel up

Volume - channel down

thought button

whatever your thinking it does

transport button

teleport to any place

erosion button

cause earth quakes

pizza delivery

whatever I want button

Kyle

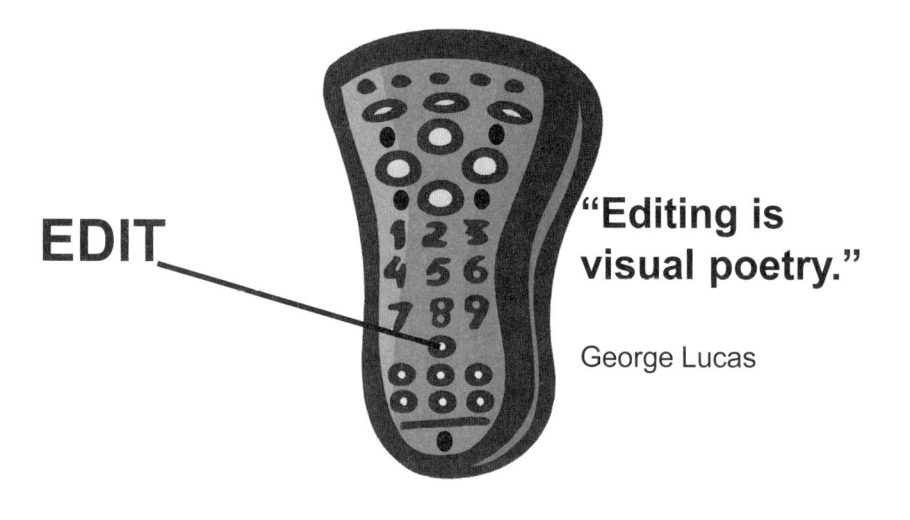

EDIT

"Editing is visual poetry."

George Lucas

"Editing is not just about finding the right picture, it's about making the choice. You can take the two kinds of editing—words and images—and make them complementary. Or you can use the same words, but choose different pictures, and the viewer will have a whole different take on what happened. The choice the editor makes becomes part of the story." Joe Wren,   Editor, KOMO 4 News, Seattle (an ABC Affiliate)

Editing is like a puzzle with a lot of different edges. In its most basic form, it is a process by which scenes are assembled. Well-chosen edits can not only tell a story, they can identify relationships, establish the whereabouts of events, alter the pace of the action, affect a mood, heighten suspense, mellow the tone, make the viewer cry, or better, laugh. Editing is artform in motion.

Nearly everything we see on screen is edited for time and content. These are business decisions, necessary to make a two-hour movie fit into a two-hour time slot, with, say, twelve minutes of commercials every hour.

But editing is far more than digitally sewing images together, or taking out parts of a scene that might offend the audience—or worse, the sponsors! Editing, now more than ever before, can shape a show and manipulate viewers. Editing can, in fact, alter audience reality.

Recently, a *Newsweek* article by Jeanne McDowell offered a behind-the-scenes look at editing's role in an American TV mainstay: "Five Tricks of Reality TV." It would seem that there are some good reasons to question the term reality TV. Is it real? Here are some edits you may not know you've seen.

1. **Frankenbiting:** This technique stitches together clips from different scenes to make the people on camera say what the makers of the show *wish* they had said. The upside is that this can clarify what a less gifted person is trying to say; the downside is that frankenbiting can actually put words in a speaker's mouth that were not said in that scene or context. (AUTHOR'S NOTE: This is **DIGITAL VENTRILOQUISM.**)

2. **Fake Settings:** According to some insiders on *The Apprentice*, the Board Room is just a regular TV studio set, not Mr. Trump's inner sanctum, as the show implies.

3. **Misleading Montage:** In the Looks Can Deceive Department, cutting to a contestant looking unhappy—for whatever reason—can make him or her seem jealous, angry, or outraged if the cut is edited into the right scene at the right time, *even if the clips were shot days apart.*

4. **The Leading Interview:** According to McDowell's article, makers rely on confessional Q & A's to fill in **when the real event didn't provide enough drama.** Questioned the right way, **contestants can make a conflict sound more dramatic than it looked on camera.**

5. **The Overdub:** Want to create some faux passion? On Fox's 2003 *Joe Millionaire,* the leading man, Evan Marriott, disappeared off-camera and into the bushes with his date, Sarah Kozer. But when the segment aired, "lusty noises and captions" were added to suggest that the couple was doing more than kissing. Kozer disagreed with the insinuation and the network.

There are other ways to alter a show through creative editing. One of the biggest wastes of audience time is the "intra-episode recap," in which we see some seconds of video from the previous segment, repeated before the beginning of any new footage. Then, there will be a preview of the next segment at the end. Sometimes, the same scene is tagged at the end of several segments in a row to "tease" the viewer into hanging on until the very end of the show. Of course, by the time the program finally comes to an end, the viewer may have sat through six showings of each recap, and there may be several recaps for each of the two or more teams. ***By the time the show ends, you may already be able to recite segments of the dialogue from memory, because you've seen them so many times!***

Without teases and recaps, you, the viewer, could probably get an unbearable hour-long show down to an almost bearable half-hour. But you wouldn't have been able to see all those commercials in between, now, would you?

Another reason for the epidemic of reality shows is basic greenery. MONEY. Take the following shows (PLEASE!): *The Apprentice, Bachelor, Bachelorette, Trading Spouses, Meet Your New Mom,* one known in the author's house as *Nightmare Nannies for Spawn of Satan,* and *Clean House* (better known as *The Attack of the Plastic Bins and People Unafraid to Use Them*). Their common denominator is they are cheap to make. There are no actors to pay and no scripts, so no writers to pay.

While you may not share the producers' artistic vision, if there is one, it should be clear that the editors are doing most of the work.

Another function of the editor is to surgically remove, sometimes on very short notice, an image or phrase that can cost the network some serious money in fines from the FCC, as you read in the button marked **DISPLAY.** This is why there is a five- to seven-second delay on most live broadcasts.

Editing can change history—if you let it.

SPONGEHEADZ: U & MEdia

In November 2005, during the annual Macy's Thanksgiving Day Parade, windy conditions blew one of the giant, human-tethered balloons into a streetlight. The post bent and debris fell on some of the parade onlookers, injuring two of them. NBC immediately switched over to video of those particular balloons *from the 2004 parade*, casually working a comment on the "file footage" into the banter between the hosts. They went back to the LIVE broadcast only after the injured people had received medical help and were hauled away from NBC cameras.

Clearly, no one—especially not the candy manufacturers!—wanted the image of two giant M & M's running amok, or worse, spilling blood ("LIVE on 5th Avenue! *WHEN CANDIES ATTACK!*") seared into the memories of the nation's children. Kids watching the NBC coverage, and many of their parents, didn't know anything had happened until much later—unless they were watching a different station. Some of you just found out a few sentences ago.

One lesson here is that "to edit" doesn't necessarily mean "to cut out." It can also mean to insert something that wasn't there originally, and digital editing makes the process much easier than old-school linear editing ever did.

Digital editing can put someone who claims to be in a meeting with a government official (CLICK) right in the picture, as that person may claim. It can just as easily remove a face from a crowded room when such a claim is denied. And with images that may be on-screen less than a few seconds, how will you ever know?

Last year some TV campaign material offered a photo of a diverse crowd listening to a politician. But a closer look at the picture showed that the audience had been carefully assembled—in groups of sixteen to twenty people—and then replicated a dozen times. (Hey, isn't that Larry? Right there? And over there? And there too? And...)

This underscores another connection between images and reading. If you watch a news show that ignores an event like a peace march, a labor rally, a teacher demonstration (for contracts, smaller class size, or more school supplies), and/or a political gathering, or one that gives you only a fraction of the number of actual participants, *and you read a completely different story about the same event from an alternative news site*, this should tell you something important: Your family needs more news options, more sites, to get a picture of the world that really is "fair and balanced." (AUTHOR'S RECOMMENDATION: Watch *BBC in America* once a day, followed by *Countdown, The Daily Show*, and *The Colbert Report*. Read the "big" papers online, but seek alternative sources for news on the Web.) Maybe then you'll have an accurate picture of life on this planet.

Hats off to the editors who put together satiric content for Comedy Central.

The current political climate, of course, gives them lots of great material, but they have managed to select the best for innovative video montages and some (hysterical) digital edits.

Comedy Central satirists Stephen Colbert and Jon Stewart have become the era's most effective media critics, drawing distinguished guests from left, right, and center, and providing a spirited place for public debate.
Jessica Clark, *In These Times*

> **These are times in which the significance and nature of jokes is a matter of debate, and in which the effort to shape public opinion by way of ridicule and satire has become a serious project.**
> Boston College Professor Paul Lewis,
> *Cracking Up: American Humor in a Time of Conflict*

Perhaps we **can** survive this election cycle—with a sense of humor.

We also need to take a firm stand against revisionist history, digital or otherwise.

In early June 2006, FOX pundit Bill O'Reilly confronted an astounded U.S. Senator John McCain with a statement that reversed some well-documented historical facts.

The Olympic-level backpedaling by O'Reilly was made worse when it was discovered that the actual transcripts of the show had been altered, leaving out O'Reilly's misstatement, and the "corrected" transcripts had been sent off to transcription services, digitized, and made available to the public—except that what the transcripts said did not match the videotape. (Once exposed, the original transcripts were returned to their original, albeit inaccurate in content, form.)

Sure, O'Reilly's rival at MSNBC had legitimate complaints with the other network, not only for the seriousness of the mistake (in which O'Reilly accused U.S. soldiers of committing a massacre in Belgium during WWII), but the insidious way that the truth of the exchange with a sitting U.S. Senator had been altered. "Bill-O," as he is known on rival MSNBC's *Countdown*, was (once again) declared that day's "Worst Person in the World." (Mr. O'Reilly achieves this status on a weekly and sometimes daily basis, although he is facing some stiff competition in pundit Ann Coulter, a.k.a. "Coultergeist.")

It comes down to this: ALWAYS ASK QUESTIONS. Look for the edits. Search for multiple sources. Make certain of the integrity of what you are watching (as was mentioned in the BALANCE chapter.) Trust is earned. Integrity is infinitely more important than spin.

And a good editor—a great editor—can be the difference between "truth" and **"truthiness."** (Thank you, Stephen Colbert!)

ZAP

1. Together, learn how to count cuts (every time the picture changes, that's an edit.) Start off with something relatively slow-paced, and do a thirty-second segment. Consider yourself in training—don't try MTV until you are truly prepared for three edits a second!

2. Editing isn't just images, it's sound. The next time you watch news with your kids, listen for "nat sound"—the natural sounds of flooding water, a volcano, farm animals, city noises, thunderstorms, fire engines, or the roar of a crowd. A good editor will try to include nat sound where it will add to a story. Also, kids immediately pick up changes in music that lead to scary scenes—show them how when the music goes minor, your minors are being prepared for…BAM!

3. Ask your kids how they would change a frequently watched show. How could they edit it to make it shorter? Or, as unlikely as this sounds, longer—or better?

hey wheres the on button button

Pizza button

Video game button

Freaky Elvis dude button

Max

DELETE

We have all had moments that we would like to delete from memory. And thankfully, we don't broadcast what's in our heads. We can be as selective as we want.

TV is not like that. How do we deal with programming we don't like?

And how do we prevent our kids from watching programs that we consider age-inappropriate? And what about other concerns?

The solution is not excess, as in, "That show is too _____." (Insert an adjective of your choice.)

It's about **access**.

You don't have to have a show banished from the airwaves. You can just make it **unavailable** at your house.

After all, the choice of programming is more about the searcher than the maker.

SPONGEHEADZ: U & MEdia

Parental controls are available in nearly every TV, as well as through cable and dish offerings. If you find some programming objectionable, raise your hand and vote with your remote. **Yours is "the hand that rocks the ratings."**

The solution to what we dislike on TV is not to have the program deleted. You already have network censors paid to monitor programming, who are unafraid, even in these times, to bring down the gavel on dialogue, story lines, and visuals they decide are "troublesome."

Learn to use the safeguards you already have available. BLOCK the programming you do not want your child to watch.

You, a highly evolved human being, have opposable thumbs and capable fingertips. You can change a channel or limit access to a specific type of programming. You can prevent all access to programming you find offensive. You can even use an abbreviation, NFU, as in, "That show is NFU (NOT FOR US.)" Just pronounce it carefully.

The airwaves are as flawed and varied as their audience—they are, after all, programmed by humans. If you are waiting for media to reach perfection, learn what the symbol for "infinity" means. (Not the logo for the luxury car, the real deal.) That's how long you'll be holding onto that remote.

Deleting a show from your personal viewing schedule (or your family's) because you find it personally offensive is easily accomplished by pushing a button. And that's cool.

Deleting the program from the publicly owned airwaves, based on your personal religious, social, or cultural beliefs is not.

That's called **CENSORSHIP**. And in a free society, it has no place.

ZAP 1. Your child has wanted to watch a particular show for some time, and your responses to the request have been "Never," "No," and "When hell freezes over." Tonight will be different. Watch a show that you have never let him or her watch, and do it together. A number of things will happen:

a) Your child can no longer complain, "But you've never even seen it! How do you know it's so terrible?"

b) Your child will crave it less because it's no longer such an enticing mystery.

c) You may find out, as some viewers of *The Simpsons* and *South Park* have, that no matter how much you are grossed out or offended (and you probably will be, at some point!), there is frequently a moral to each story. Homer always learns some kind of life lesson. (OK, and Kenny almost always dies, but there is usually a lesson about intolerance or hypocrisy.) By shredding stereotypes in an equal-opportunity-insulting environment, we learn to recognize our own negative biases.

That's why, in 2006, *South Park* won the prestigious Peabody Award!

2. Now that you have made this gesture, trade off and ask your child to watch something with you, a show YOU really want to see. Best bets: A & E, Discovery Channel, the History Channel, TVLand, and Animal Planet. (The author prefers cheesy, ancient sci-fi—but it is an acquired taste.)

3. Talk about the reasons a show has been cancelled—especially if it was a family favorite. Who wanted it off the air *and why?* Then send a letter or e-mail to the local station that carried the program, expressing the views, agreeing or disagreeing, of all family members.

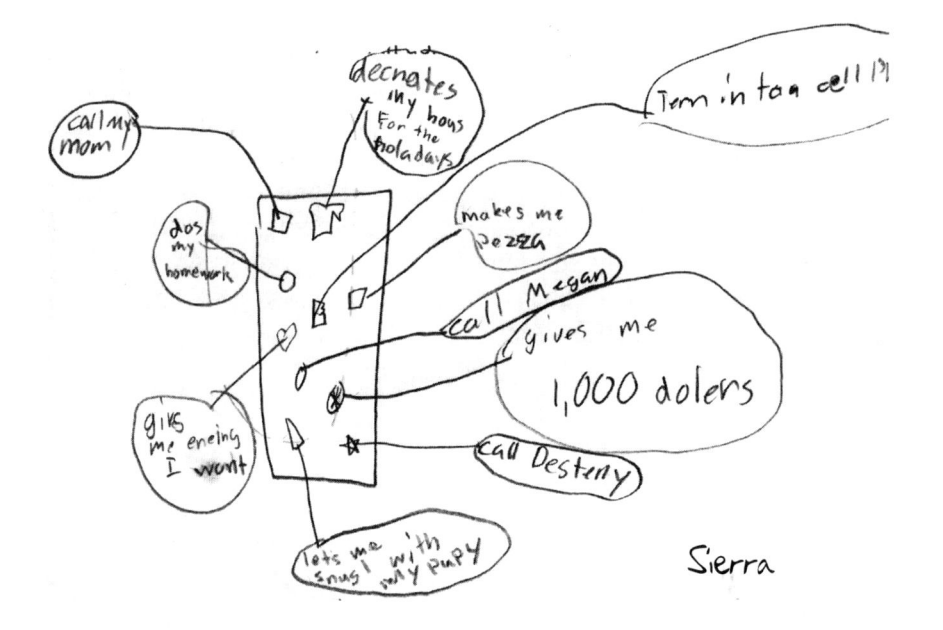

call my mom

decnates my hous For the holadays

Tom in too cell!?!

dos my homework

makes me pezza

call Megan

gives me 1,000 dolers

giks me eneing I wont

call Desteny

lets me snusl with my pupy

Sierra

REV/REW

Entire books have been written about where TV has been. Treating this chapter simply as an historical reference would not do this complicated medium any justice.

The best map to the media landscape is available as a TV TIMELINE and can be downloaded for free at **www.acmecoalition.org/media**. It is reproduced here to alert you to the fact that our 230-year-old country has been dealing with media here since 1796, not long after the American "experiment" began.

I watch TV for relaxation, because you can rest and it doesn't take that much energy. And for curiosity, because I really want to see what's gonna happen in shows like COPS and Fear Factor.
Spencer, grade 6

U.S. MEDIA LANDSCAPE TIMELINE (selective events and innovations)

YEAR	Transportation, Communications, & Digital Technology	Memorabilia, Portraits, Buttons, Banners, & Signs	Print Material, Photography, Newspapers & Magazines	Music, Film, Radio & Television
Prior to 1796	Direct mail 1789 Bill of Rights establishes freedom of the press 1733 Invention of the cotton gin	Memorabilia (ribbons, images on china) Posters & banners Paintings & drawings Painted portraits	Handbills, pamphlets & books Printed political cartoons (woodcuts or engravings) 1787-88 Federalist Papers first published as newspaper editorials 1787-95 Most newspapers partisan weeklies 1796 Thomas Paine's The Age of Reason 1798-1800 Increase from 51 to 83 Democratic-Republican newspapers	Political songs & sheet music
1796	1796 Invention of lithography (made printmaking quick & easy) 1798 Passage of the Sedition Act	1796 Metal tokens		
1800		1800 Hats with twigs, bucktails or cockades		
1804	1807 Launching of first steamboat	1804 Ceramic pitchers with candidate's likeness		
1808		1808 Inlaid Sheffield razors with political slogans		
1812			1814 First photographic image (camera obscura)	1814 Francis Scott Key writes "The Star Spangled Banner"
1816	1817 Begin construction of the Erie Canal			
1820	1820s-1830s Development of canal system			
1824	1824 Erie Canal completed 1825 First railroad in the U.S.	1824 Metal lucky tokens, bandanas, snuff boxes, thread boxes & combs supporting Jackson	1825 First published campaign biography (Andrew Jackson) 1826 United States Telegraph newspaper (supporting Jackson) 1827 First African American newspaper, Freedom's Journal 1828 Webster's American Dictionary of the English Language published	1824 Ludlow's "The Hunters of Kentucky" song published celebrating Jackson's victory at New Orleans
1828	1828-31 Price of paper falls 25% 1829 Invention of the typewriter early 1830s First use of steam-powered cylinder press in the U.S.	1828 Hickory Sticks become first symbol used to represent a presidential candidate (Jackson)		
1832			1833 "Penny Press" begins with publication of The New York Sun 1835 de Tocqueville publishes Democracy in America 1837 First fixed photographic image that didn't fade (daguerreotype)	
1836		1837 Satirical paper banknotes & copper medalets mocking Jackson		
1840		1840 Log Cabin imagery on a wide range of memorabilia 1840 Pull cards 1840 Whig "Rolling Ball" 1840 Parade flags & standards	1841 Horace Greeley starts The New York Tribune	
1844	1844 Wood pulp paper invented (vastly reduces cost of newspapers) 1844 Invention of the telegraph		1847 Frederick Douglass publishes The North Star in Rochester, NY (rise of abolitionist press)	

U.S. MEDIA LANDSCAPE TIMELINE (selective events and innovations)

YEAR	Transportation, Communications, & Digital Technology	Memorabilia, Portraits, Buttons, Banners, & Signs	Print Material, Photography, Newspapers & Magazines	Music, Film, Radio & Television
1848	1846 Rotary press invented (for rapid printing of newspapers) 1850s Rise of railroads (miles of track triples in 10 years)		1848 Associated Press formed in NY 1851 *The Nation* (oldest still publishing magazine) 1851 *The New York Times* founded 1852 *Uncle Tom's Cabin* published 1853 First news photograph (daguerreotype)	
1852				
1856	1856 Western Union begins	1856 Ferrotype & cardboard photos on brass tokens or pins	1857 *Harper's Weekly*	
1860	1861 First U.S. transcontinental telegraph	1860 Split rail imagery on a wide range of memorabilia (Lincoln) 1860 Torchlight parades	1860 First use of engravings from photographs on political ribbons & prints 1861 First Thomas Nast political cartoons 1863-65 Civil War photographs	
1864	1866 Transcontinental telegraph cable			
1868	1869 Transcontinental railroad completed		1869 First "dime" novels 1870 Begin explosion of newspaper circulation (increases 900% by 1910) 1873 First color photographs	
1872				
1876	1876 Invention of telephone 1876 Invention of celluloid 1877 Invention of the phonograph 1878 Invention of dry plate photography 1879 Invention of incandescent light bulb			
1880	1880 NYC streets lit by electricity 1882 First electric-power station (NYC) 1883 Half-tone screen invented (for mass reproduction of images)	1880 First use of gaudy lapel studs with candidate's picture	1880 First articles about possibility of television published in *Scientific American*	
1884	1884 Invention of Nipkow scanning disk (earliest form of television)		1884 *Huckleberry Finn* published	
1888	1888 Invention of the kinetoscope (first moving pictures)	1888 "Turkey red" bandanas (Grover Cleveland campaign)	1888 Invention of Kodak box camera with transparent celluloid film	late 1880s First peep shows & nickelodeons
1892	1891 First wireless telegraphy 1895 Marconi invents radio telegraphy	1892 Candidate images on thread, pincushions, trivets	1890s-early 1900s Muckrakers expose corporate & manufacturing scandals	

U.S. MEDIA LANDSCAPE TIMELINE (selective events and innovations)

YEAR	Transportation, Communications, & Digital Technology	Memorabilia, Portraits, Buttons, Banners, & Signs	Print Material, Photography, Newspapers & Magazines	Music, Film, Radio & Television
1896	1896 First "whistle-stop" campaign (William Jennings Bryan) 1896 Tabulating Machine Company (later becomes IBM) 1899 Invention of magnetic tape recorder 1900 First transmission of human speech via radio waves	1896 Memorabilia in gold & silver 1896 First celluloid pin back campaign buttons 1896 Placards on moveable wheels	1890s cheap color newspaper, "yellow journalism" 1897 First published photographs in newspapers (New York Tribune) 1897 Saturday Evening Post begins 1898 First photographs taken with artificial light	1894 Invention of motion picture camera 1896 Edison develops vitascope movies (shown on large screen with musical accompaniment) 1897 First newsreels shown
1900	1902 Invention of photoelectric scanning for image transfer 1902-03 Invention of the vacuum tube (wireless sound) 1903 First airplane flight (Wright brothers at Kitty Hawk)	early 1900s Stereographic 3-D cards and "lantern slides" 1900 First penny postcards used for political purposes	1900 First mass marketed Browning cameras	
1904	1906 Ford produces first automobiles 1906 First "offset" presses built	1903 First Teddy Bears (named after Pres. Theodore Roosevelt) 1904 Teddy Bear imagery on a wide range of memorabilia	1906 Introduction of Autochrome color photography 1907 First daily comic strip ("Mr. Mutt")	1906 First radio program broadcast by Reginald Fessenden 1907 Lee De Forest becomes the first DJ (broadcasts from lower Manhattan)
1908		1908 Political watchfobs		
1912	1912 Titanic sinks, reported by ship to shore radio telegraphy 1914 Federal Trade Commission began (regulating false advertising)			
1916	1914 First assembly line production (Ford)		1913-14 First 35 mm cameras	1915 Birth of a Nation (3 hour film) (beginning of modern movie industry) 1916 First political polls by Literary Digest 1919 RCA formed 1919 New York Illustrated Daily News (first tabloid newspaper in the U.S.) 1919 Creation of United Artists (first film studio)
1920	1920s Technologies to improve train & air travel: radial engine, pressurized cabins, diesel-electric engine, electronics, plastics 1920s Rise of electric appliances (refrigerators, washing machines, irons, vacuum cleaners) which revolutionizing housework 1922 Motion Picture Association (first regulation of film industry) 1922 First Pulitzer prize for a political cartoon	1920 First mass produced lithographed tin buttons 1920 Political decals for car windows 1920s Electric glass window signs	1920s Rise of wire services, so nationally syndicated stories 1920s Newspapers begin being absorbed into national chains	1920 First radio station (KDKA) begins broadcasting in Pittsburgh 1920 First radio broadcast of results of a presidential election 1920s-1930s Rise of jazz and dance halls, Harlem Renaissance 1921 Reader's Digest 1922 First commercial on radio

U.S. MEDIA LANDSCAPE TIMELINE (selective events and innovations)

YEAR	Transportation, Communications, & Digital Technology	Memorabilia, Portraits, Buttons, Banners, & Signs	Print Material, Photography, Newspapers & Magazines	Music, Film, Radio & Television
1924	1923 National Association of Broadcasters mid-1920s Advertising "comes of age" mid-1920s Proliferation of telephones 1924 IBM formed 1927 Federal Radio Act	1924 License plate attachments	1923 *Time* magazine 1925 *The New Yorker* 1927 Invention of modern flashbulb	1923 First weekly radio commentaries 1927 First national radio network (NBC) 1927 First feature-length motion picture with sound (*The Jazz Singer*) 1927 First experimental broadcasts of TV late 1920s Cartoon shorts in movie theaters 1929 "Happy Days are Here Again" published 1930 Almost every home has radio
1928	early 1930s Earliest analog computer developed			1930 First daily 15-minute radio newscast 1932 Breaking news story on radio, interrupting regularly scheduled programming (Lindbergh baby)
1932	1934 Federal Communications Act (regulating radio, TV, telephones & telegraph)	1932 Oilcloth covers for spare tires with political messages & images	1933 *Newsweek* magazine	1933 First radio "Fireside Chat" by Roosevelt
1936	late 1930s Rural electrification program (part of New Deal) late 1930s Rural road construction (allows timely delivery of newspapers)		1935 First comic books 1936 *Life* magazine	mid-1930s First radio soap operas 1937 Live radio broadcast of the Hindenburgh disaster 1937 First feature-length animated film (*Snow White*) 1938 Orson Welles radio broadcast of "War of the Worlds" 1938 First regular daily newsbroadcast on radio ("World Today") 1938 First radio quiz shows 1939 Television broadcasts from the New York World's Fair 1939 FDR is first president shown on TV 1939-1945 Live broadcasts of the war by Edward R. Murrow
1940	1941 FCC Mayflower Doctrine (broadcasters can't be advocates) 1942 Office of War Information established by Roosevelt to coordinate propaganda and information services 1942 War Advertising Council established to raise money for the war effort using popular stars	1940 First political billboards		late 1930s First films in color 1941 First commercial television broadcast

U.S. MEDIA LANDSCAPE TIMELINE (selective events and innovations)

YEAR	Transportation, Communications, & Digital Technology	Memorabilia, Portraits, Buttons, Banners, & Signs	Print Material, Photography, Newspapers & Magazines	Music, Film, Radio & Television
1944	1946 First mainframe computer invented			1945 Radio networks banned advertising for 4 days during coverage of President Roosevelt's death 1948 4 commercial TV networks 1948 TV received in only 47 cities 1948 First televised conventions
1948	1948-1955 Begin decline of passenger trains 1948 Last whistle stop campaign (Truman) early 1950s Rise of suburbs leads to huge increase in cars 1950 Invention of color television		1948 First Polaroid instant cameras	
1952	1952 First computerized election predictions	1952 Wide range of memorabilia in political campaigns (stickers, handkerchiefs, matchbooks, etc.)		1952 *Today* show begins 1952-1956 Begin decline in radio use 1952-1954 Number of TV stations grow from 108 to 356 in 2 years 1952 First political TV commercials 1952 First 30 minute paid political messages 1952 Nixon's "Checkers" speech 1954 Army-McCarthy hearings on *See It Now*
1956	1956-1962 Begin construction of interstate highways 1956-1960 Increased commercial air travel	1956 First bumper stickers used for political campaigns		
1960	1962 First transatlantic satellite transmissions			1960 Almost 90% of homes have TV sets 1960 First televised presidential debates 1960 Evening news expands from 15 to 30 minutes
1964	1965 Launch of first commercial communications satellite	1964 Cowboy hats used to support LBJ		1963 End of newsreels in theaters 1963 3-day TV coverage of Kennedy assassination and funeral 1964 Most TV broadcasts in color 1964 First televised war coverage (on film, delayed)
1968	1967 First handheld calculator 1967 Public Broadcasting Act 1969-83 Internet begins as ARPANET early 1970s Invention of the VCR 1971 Invention of the microprocessor 1971 Federal Election Campaign Act	late 1960s First T-shirts with peace signs & anti-war messages	1969 *The Selling of the President 1968* published 1970 First *Doonesbury* political cartoons	1968 *60 Minutes* begins on CBS 1968 TV coverage of riots outside the Democratic Convention in Chicago 1968 Presidential candidate Nixon appears on *Laugh-In* 1969 Apollo 11 transmits live TV pictures from the moon 1969 PBS begins broadcasting 1971 National Public Radio begins 1972 HBO (first subscription cable channel)
1972	1972 First television-based home computer games		1972 *Washington Post* uncovers Watergate Scandal	1973-4 TV coverage of the Watergate hearings

U.S. MEDIA LANDSCAPE TIMELINE (selective events and innovations)

YEAR	Transportation, Communications, & Digital Technology	Memorabilia, Portraits, Buttons, Banners, & Signs	Print Material, Photography, Newspapers & Magazines	Music, Film, Radio & Television
1976	1975 First fiber-optics transmissions			1974 All the President's Men published 1974 Nixon announces resignation in live TV speech 1975 Good Morning America begins 1975 Star Wars coins term "Evil Empire" 1975 Saturday Night Live debuts 1979 C-SPAN cable network begins
1980	late 1970s Rise of Political Action Committees (PACs) 1977 First affordable personal computers (by Apple & Commodore) 1979 Invention of the mobile cellular phone 1980 Michael Deaver named "Ad Man of the Year" for Reagan campaign 1980 First supermarket scanners in use 1981 First laptop computers 1982 Compact Disk invented 1983 Begin commercial & popular use of the Internet (e.g., e-mail)		early 1980s First digital manipulation of photographs 1982 USA Today begins publishing	1980 Cable News Network (CNN) begins 1981 MTV begins broadcasting 1981 Televised release of American hostages from Iran 1983 Frontline debuts on PBS
1984	1984 Apple Macintosh 1985 Microsoft Windows 1986 Nintendo Video Games 1987 Reagan suspends the Fairness Doctrine (requiring equal time for controversial issues)	1984 Hugely popular buttons supporting Geraldine Ferraro (first female VP candidate from a major party)		1986 Iran-Contra hearings on TV
1988	1988 Children's Television Act passed regulating children's TV (vetoed) 1988 Begin to use focus groups/dial groups to judge responses to political speeches 1990 Children's Television Act, revised, passed by Congress early 1990s First Direct Satellite dish broadcasts		1991 First professional digital camera systems (for photojournalists)	1988 Rush Limbaugh TV show debuts 1988 Fox Channel debuts (first new successful broadcast network since 1940s) 1989 Berlin Wall torn down, covered by live television 1991 Desert Storm bombing of Baghdad broadcast live by CNN 1991 Rodney King beating by police officers shown on Today show.
1992	1992-1996 Media begin "Ad Watches" judging accuracy of political ads 1993 World Wide Web created 1993 First Palm Pilots introduced 1993 First search engines			1992 First town-hall meeting style presidential debate 1995 O.J. Simpson trial broadcast live & aftermath (riots, looting in Los Angeles)
1996	1998-2000 Media highlight Y2K fears 1998 Google debuts online 1999 MP3 makes music downloads possible 1999 First weblogs (start of "blogging")			1996 The O'Reilly Factor debuts on Fox 1996 MSNBC debuts 1997 Introduction of DVDs 1998 Digital TV broadcasting begins

Lynn Ziegler

U.S. MEDIA LANDSCAPE TIMELINE (selective events and innovations)

YEAR	Transportation, Communications, & Digital Technology	Memorabilia, Portraits, Buttons, Banners, & Signs	Print Material, Photography, Newspapers & Magazines	Music, Film, Radio & Television
2000	2000-2004 Micromarketing increases 2002 TiVO digital recording system 2002-2004 Rise of video and news on the web 2003-2004 Rise of "blogging" 2003 FCC votes to reduce limits on media consolidation			1998-99 Coverage of Monica Lewinsky scandal & Clinton impeachment trial 1999 *The West Wing* debuts on NBC 2000 Major networks erroneously announce Gore elected president 2001 Live TV coverage of Sept. 11 events 2001 Live coverage of War in Afghanistan 2001-2004 Rise of *Clear Channel* radio network 2002 *NOW with Bill Moyers* debuts on PBS 2003-04 Al Jazeera broadcasts Sadam Hussein statements 2003 Live coverage of War in Iraq with "embedded" reporters 2004 Film *Fahrenheit 9/11* debuts
2004				

45

Lynn Ziegler

The best way to show our kids what TV has looked like in the past is to revisit some of that programming. You can do so by tuning in to *Turner Classic, TVLand,* or going online or to the library to access video archives and old recordings.

The History Channel and the FCC Web site are excellent resources as well. Keep in mind that at some point in the future, your kids will look back at the shows you watch this week, or even tonight, as "the good old days."

 1. Plan a visit—virtual or real—to the nearest Museum of Radio and Television.

2. Do some research and find out which TV station in your town has been on-air the longest. Contact the community outreach person and ask what early programming is available for classroom use. You may be able to find someone to come and speak to your child's class. Or you can arrange a class tour of the TV station, which most kids (even teenagers) really enjoy.

3. Contact the National Association of Television Arts and Sciences (NATAS) in your area. They will be a valuable source of information for your trip "backwards in time."

Any sufficiently advanced technology is indistinguishable from magic.
Sci-Fi Wizard Arthur C. Clark

There are two ways to live life. One is as though nothing were a miracle. The other is as if *everything* were a miracle.
Albert Einstein

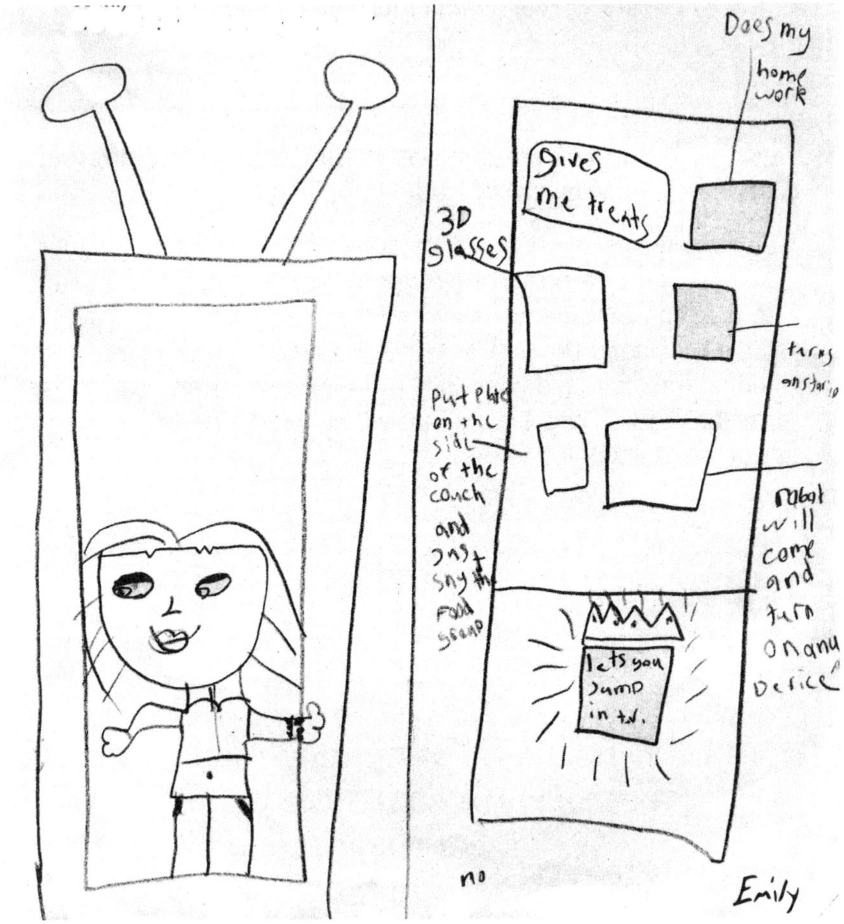
Does my home work
gives me treats
3D glasses
turns
Put plate on the side of the couch
robot will come and turn on any device
lets you jump in t.v.
no
Emily

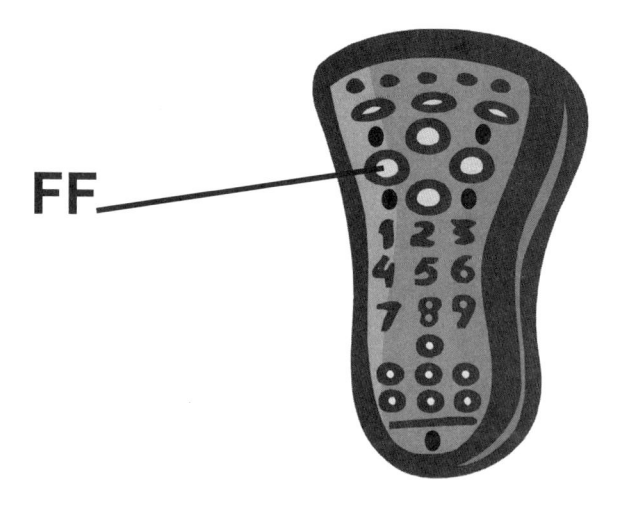

FF

There *are* a few things that can be guaranteed about your TV. The first is that it is going to change. The next is that you will not be able to anticipate what that change will look like until after it happens. Television will surprise you.

This isn't just about technology—changes there are a given. This is about how we choose to get what we see—access (and probably, excess) again.

The risk of writing this chapter is that there are infinitely more items and developments than can appear here already in the techno-pipeline (not TUBES, Senator Stevens!) Hopefully, none will be obsolete before this book reaches you.

ANALOG 2 DIGITAL

With TV on FAST FORWARD (as it has always been!) a major change will take place as we go from analog TV to digital. The picture on the screen may get clearer, but your picture of the industry may be a bit murky. Here is the latest on the coming blackout of analog.

First of all, the House of Representatives has set a deadline of December 31, 2009, for the cutoff of analog services and the complete changeover to digital. Consumer groups are already asking that the cost of a digital transformer (like a cable box) be picked up by the government, so that millions of people are not cut off from the airwaves that are rightfully theirs.

Here are some issues to watch:

In 2006, the current Republican bill covers only ten million of the possible twenty million households (or more) that would go blank after analog goes away and would do so on a "first come, first served" basis.

The bipartisan Senate bill allocates $3 billion for a subsidy that covers EVERY TV VIEWING HOUSEHOLD.

The House version requires viewers to seek out the subsidy themselves—and only puts $960 million towards it. The Senate bill dates the turnover for 2009. Part of the problem of subsidizing boxes for viewers is that the House bill returns the auction receipts (from the spectrum that will be sold off) to the Treasury—rather than subsidizing the digital transition FIRST, which, according to Senator Markey (D-MA) would benefit the poor and the elderly.

As was mentioned earlier, what parents need to understand is that TV's switch to digital frees up bandwidths. This means that first responders, (firefighters, police, and EMTs) **can have their own means to contact each other,** in order to avoid the communications breakdowns that plagued the tragedies of the attack on the WTC and the devastation of Katrina/Wilma/Rita/levee failure in the Gulf States.

VOD (VIDEO ON DEMAND)

VOD has the potential to bring SEISMIC change to the entertainment industry. Being able to choose from a menu of films—and not have to get in the car to go get them—has immense appeal to parents who are trying to cut down on mileage. But travel issues aside, VOD is revolutionizing TV because **YOU ARE CREATING THE CONTENT AND THE SCHEDULE.**

DVRs

Advertisers have always feared that use of the DVR, like the VCR, would automatically mean that audience members would skip commercials. Current research indicates that may not be the case. Consumers may actually be *attracted* to advertising that's done in a unique, creative way, especially for high-interest, new technology items.

According to *Advertising Age,* as of August 2006, 11.2 percent of households use DVRs and that number will continue to rise. People with DVRs tend to be frequent Internet users, and readers of multiple magazines, according to the same article. The study found that households with DVRs tend to be considered "affluent." But DVR usage is becoming more and more mainstream, as cable and satellite companies are making it more affordable and easy.

Along with VOD, DVRs are leading the way to an approach to watching TV called "time-shifting," and it seems to be here to stay.

MobiTV, MOBISODES

For about a $10 fee per month, you can watch TV on your cell phone. Different carriers have different names and prices for the service, and yes, you can expect to see commercials there. The best, most accurate catch-phrase for watching small (in size and time) segments is "video-snacking"—and that little space on your phone has morphed into "the third screen."

PODCASTS and RSS FEEDS

You can download programming to your computer, mobile phone, or your MP3/iPod so that you can watch/listen to the particular show while you are doing something else—walking, commuting, traveling, or exercising. The third screen, like many other facets of your life, is portable.

SATELLITE RADIO

As we go to print, the two major satellite radio offerings, SIRIUS and XM, are available as a subscription service, and you need to buy a special receiver to tune in. This means no longer driving in and out of range of smaller stations (as interesting or painfully annoying as that can sometimes be.) The clarity, plus the wide variety of noncommercial niche programming available, makes this a real growth industry.

But as we went to print, news came that XM will have an arrangement with Google to insert advertising in nonmusical channels...satellite radio may not be commercial-free for long.

Satellite radio is another way for media luminaries to expand and enhance a growing, or grown, audience. Oprah Winfrey, one of the powerful trio of women who created Oxygen Network (along with Marcy Carsey and Gerri Laybourne of Nickelodeon and ABC), has headed into space, along with Howard Stern and Air America. (Not together, of course!)

A recent article by Marc Fisher in *WaPo* (the *Washington Post)* breaks it down:

> Baseball fan: XM. Football nut: Sirius. Movie maven: XM. Howard Stern addict: Sirius. Bob Dylan freak: XM. NPR lover: Sirius. Movie soundtracks and interviews of composers who write them (like Danny Elfman and Randy Newman): XM. Playboy Radio or Korean language programming: Sirius. Only black talk show: XM.

> XM has signed Bob Dylan, Snoop Dogg and Oprah. Sirius' stars: Martha Stewart, Deepak Chopra, Judith Regan and Mark Cuban.

But while both services vie for big names, the main attraction on XM (6.9 million subscribers) and Sirius (4.7 million subscribers) is the

music. The tunes are often similar; how they're presented is the difference. According to Marc Fisher, the original vision has "yielded to a more mainstream approach." XM dropped cocktail lounge sounds, African pop, and free-form exotic music; Sirius silenced swing jazz, baroque classics, and tropical and calypso music. (Both companies killed their world music channels, which were eclectic mixes of tunes from every continent.)

Sirius has NPR; XM has Air America. For more information from this piece, go to **www.washingtonpost.com**.

BUS RADIO

Talk about a captive audience! This year, school buses across many states will be able to offer high-interest kids' programming en route to classes. And LOTS of commercials. (Think of this as Channel One, to the soundtrack of "The Wheels on the Bus"—*not* good news.) If your school district has not yet authorized (or "discovered") this plan, see what you can do to put the brakes on it.

VONGO

This is a service that enables you to download recent commercial film releases to your computer. By the time you read this, it's likely to have a number of competitive siblings.

"BINGE-VIEWING"

You can watch an entire season of a favorite show in a marathon motif—all in one night or one weekend by renting or buying the DVD of that program.

This enables you to watch a show that you may not have noticed, but which has suddenly become a hot property. You can also watch and keep shows you wish hadn't been cancelled and view them any time you like. This is the TV equivalent of renting all of the *Star Wars* films to watch chronologically or the *Back to the Future* trilogy, one after the other. It has become a relatively popular, inexpensive party mode for young adults (add pizza) and kids, especially in bad weather—provided that the electricity stays on. (The author recommends the Monty Python boxed set, especially after a life crisis. Think of it as digital therapy. Keep laughing.)

QUBO

In September 2006, NBC, along with Telemundo, I-Network Scholastic Media, Classic Media/Big Idea, and Corus Entertainment, plans to launch this brand of kids Saturday morning programming. Unfortunately, it will replace the three-hour Discovery Channel block of shows. According to Marc Graboff, the new president of NBC Universal Television West Coast, Qubo will offer *Veggie Tales* and other programs (with theme park tie-ins*),* "But it won't be 'broccoli TV.' " Stay tuned.

PAUSE

BITZ & BYTES

Do you have a kid who would do anything to avoid opening a book? As we mentioned in "PAGE," cell phone companies in Japan are already making it possible to read books by cell phone, and the trend is headed here.

Want to watch TV anywhere? Check out the Slingbox, a network add-on from newcomer Sling Media. That will enable TV fans to view their content wirelessly from any notebook in the home or on the road. The Slingbox redirects not only live TV, but content recorded on PVRs (portable video recorders) to anywhere a broadband connection is available.

And we do mean anywhere. You may have a small TV in or near the kitchen, but the hybrid some people have always dreamed of has finally arrived—**an LCD TV screen <u>built into the refrigerator</u>**. But even there, in your refrigerator, you can't escape commercials: CBS has made a deal with the service that stamps eggs with an expiration date to ink small program promos on the egg shells, such as "'*Crack the Case*' on CBS." And no, as Miles O'Brien of CNN just **had** to say, "This is not a *yolk.*"

Many cable news network shows and broadcast organizations regularly feature segments on the latest technological advances. However, before you invest in any of these new toys, check out *Consumer Reports* at a library or online.

I don't know what the best
thing about TV is, but the worst thing
abut TV is my brother.
He decides what's on.
Allison, grade 3

 1. Go online, and Google "new electronics gadgets." At this writing, there are more than twenty-seven million entries. Knock yourself out.

2. Ask your kids to invent a gadget of their own. You have probably looked at the futuristic remote controls, drawn by elementary school students, throughout this book. These items have features unique to each artist (if you missed some of the finer points, go back and check them out again.)

3. Do some research on the most important innovations of this new century. In 2006, the remote turns fifty. Students who started college this year have never known life without a remote, or a microwave oven, let alone TV!

See what's headed your way…and try not to flinch.

Garrett

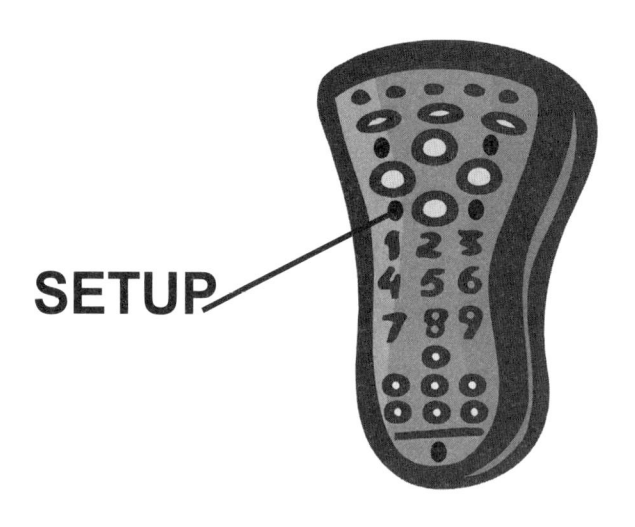

SETUP

Media are becoming more portable than ever before.

In the 1950s, TV dinners, the brainchild of the late, great Gerry Thomas, were intended to bring the family together around the gray-toned, and then the cobalt-colored electronic fireplace. Now, of course, thanks to the third screen, TV goes everywhere. (Symbologist John Fraim, a consultant on *The Da Vinci Code,* thinks feminism may owe some of its early success to "liberation from cooking" by way of the small, silver aluminum tray in front of the small, silver TV screen.)

While parents may drool over the latest big-screen (coming in 2007: 107 inches!), our kids are accustomed to watching very tiny screens for long periods of time, thanks to the video game industry in all of its incarnations.

So what is the ideal setup for people who want to get the most out of media?

Limit distractions, and maximize your focus. No matter what size screen you are looking at, it can bring you the world.

ZAP 1. Want a healthy SETUP? In the room where you watch TV most often together, BE PRE-PARED. Have a pitcher full of water and some cups on hand, and keep some healthy munchies ready in the refrigerator. This means keeping a nice fruit bowl (or other heart-friendly snacks) near the remote (along with your copy of this book.)

2. ALWAYS have a clock in the TV room. Keep an eye on the timepiece, so you can accurately say, "You have been watching TV for three hours. Please go read for a while, or listen to music." Or, "You have some sort of root growing out of your foot, looking for nourishment in the carpet. Please get up and MOVE before the SCI-FI Channel turns you into a mini-series." Whatever works.

3. Whenever possible, keep a log of what you're watching and when. Just as dieters are astounded by the foods they find themselves eating without thinking, a TV Diary can show your family the HUGE CHUNKS OF TIME spent (eaten, or for SPONGEHEADZ, ABSORBED) in front of the TV. ASK: What else could all of you be learning or doing?

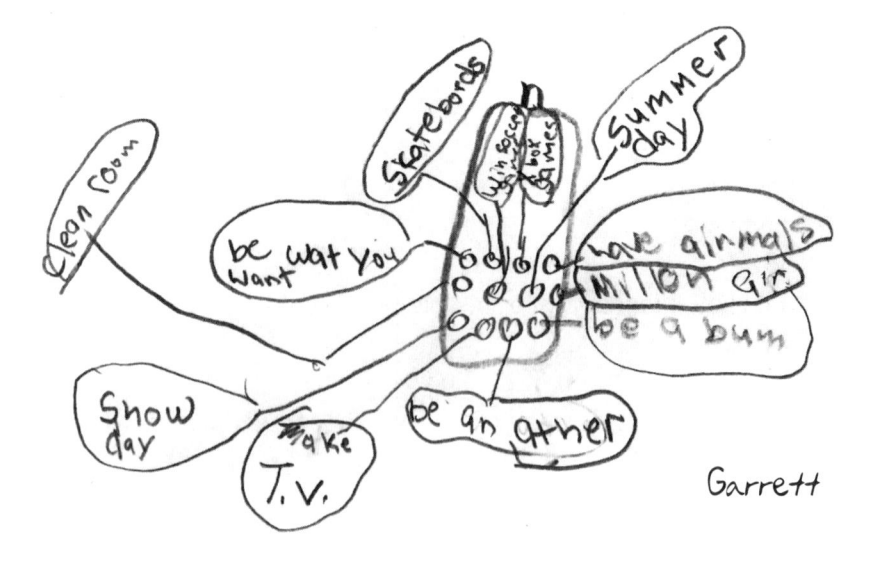

Garrett

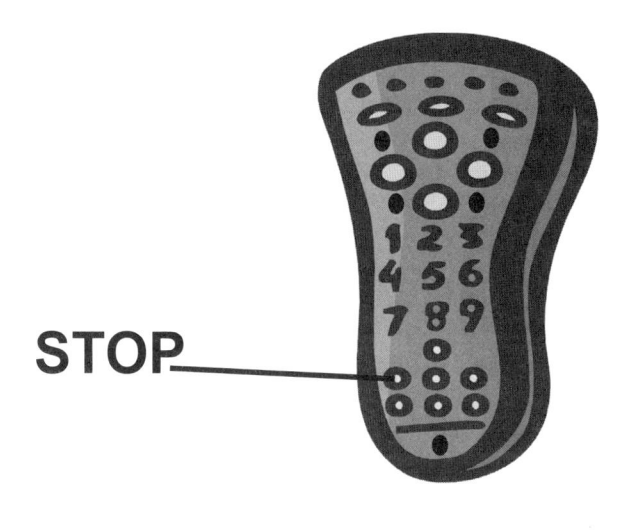

STOP

In the interests of the mental and physical health of your family, please consider doing this:

Stop BLOVIATING.

This is a public service announcement.

The days of shouting each other down are over. In these times, there has never been a greater need for that four-letter word defining "social intercourse:

Learn to exchange ideas and opinions while actively listening to the other view. Keep judgmental comments, ego-enhancers, and personal put-downs out of bounds. With two sets of elections on the horizon, learning the difference between talking and BLOVIATING may just save what's left of your family's collective sanity by those Two November Tuesdays ('06 and '08.)

In the unlikely event that you have doubts about the wisdom of this suggestion, please tune in to the *Daily Show With Jon Stewart.* He and his mostly male cohorts (hang in there, Samantha Bee!) offer proof positive that bloviating is best when you acknowledge its down-right laughability. How?

The Daily Show has a segment in which children read the actual dialogue spewed by pundits on topical talk shows. Nothing quite illuminates playground politics like seeing a three- or four-kid panel tossing adult insults, put downs, partisan observations, and other wild or unreasonable ravings at each other, just like the "big kids do." (Note to Jon Stewart: As the elections get closer, consider making this a daily segment of *The Daily Show. **PLEASE**.*)

You, dear reader, are encouraged to contact every show that features Shouters, not Commentators. OK, CNN's *Crossfire* is already off the air. However, Tony Blankley and Pat Buchanan of *The McLaughlin Group*—once described to the author by her children as "that show you watch every week where those old white guys in suits yell at each other"—yes, Eleanor, we know you're there too, and that you only yell when "the boys" don't let you get a word in!—are waiting to hear from you. If you've had a similar reaction to the show, you can contact Oliver Productions in Washington, D.C., at **www.mclaughlin.com**.

NOTE: The author will be waiting excitedly for her invitation to discuss *SPONGEHEADZ: U & MEdia* with the author of *O'Reilly For Kids* (along with his inclusion in several parts of this book) in an appearance on his show on FOX and to offer sisterhood and support to Eleanor Clift any time *The McLaughlin Group* invites her.

ZAP 1. Read the editorial page of your local paper, and then read some editorials at the national level. Don't just acknowledge that people are arguing—FIND OUT WHY! And read the new report on Sunday (talk) shows *Meet The Press, This Week With George Stephanopolis*, and *Face The Nation* for an eye-opening look at balanced opinion—or the lack of it. Add to your Sunday lineup CNN's *On the Story* and Howard Kurtz's *Reliable Sources* media analysis, CBS's *Face the Nation*, PBS's *NOW,* and of course *The McLaughlin Group.* Or you can watch Wolf Blitzer edit the best of each for his show at high noon on CNN.

2. Does your local station ever offer editorial comments at the end of a news program? Then, by law, they have to offer a chance for a viewer's rebuttal. Get your facts straight, and call them, either in support of, or especially in disagreement with, the issue in the commentary.

3. Is there an issue that your family cares passionately about?

   Contact your local children's radio station, and encourage your kids to speak up. Then call your favorite radio talk show, and, as Madonna says, "Express yourself." Your opinion counts just as much as everyone else's!

   Don't just watch talk shows that reflect your own viewpoint. Watch and listen to what "the other side" is saying,

I watch TV because I'm curious
about the world.
Bonnie, grade 4

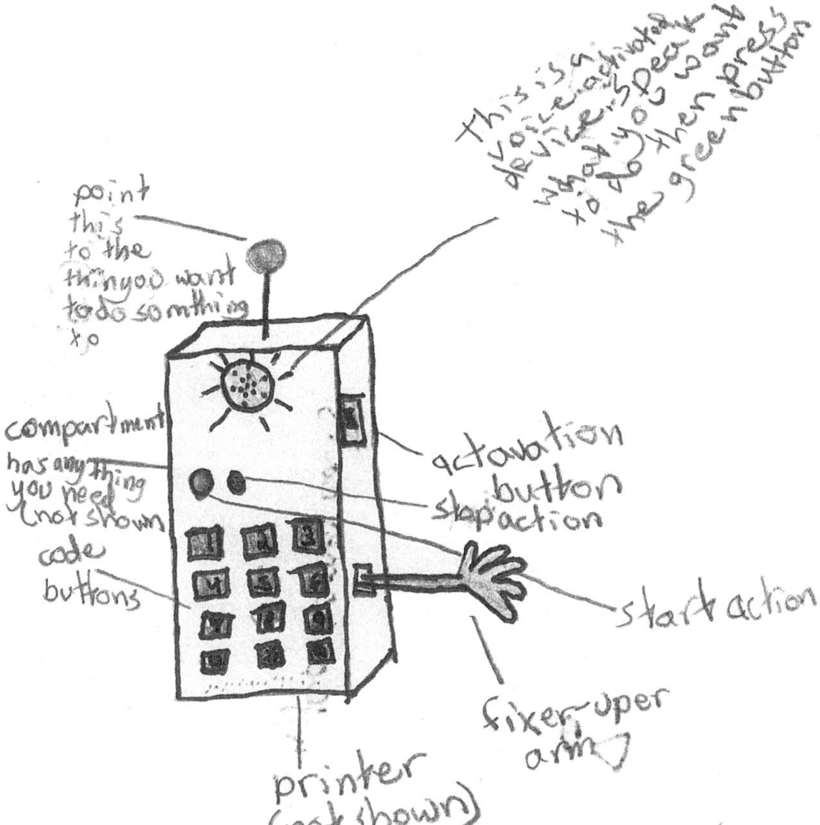

This is a voice-activated device. Speak what you want to do then press the green button

point this to the thing you want to do something to

compartment has anything you need (not shown)

code buttons

activation button
stop action

start action

fixer-uper arm

printer (not shown)

Unsigned

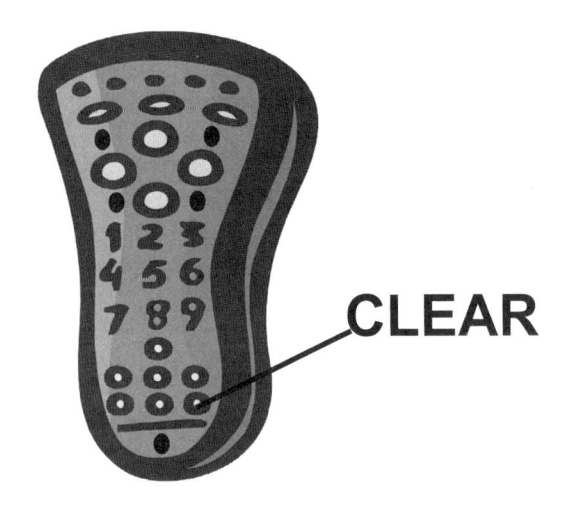

CLEAR

Let's be "clear" about something important: **SCIENCE**.

Great visuals can explain the most difficult and obscure scientific ideas and processes. In fact, after seeing a PBS program by Jean-Michel Cousteau (son of the late underwater explorer and SCUBA inventor Jacques), the President "popped up from his front row seat after the screening, congratulated the filmmaker, and urged his White House staff to 'get moving' on protecting these waters." (Source: *LA Times*, 6.15.06)

"He was enthusiastic," Cousteau said. "The show had a major impact on him, the way my father's shows had on so many people. I think he really made a discovery—a connection between the quality of our lives and the oceans."

This was a surprise move by the Bush administration, which five years earlier had considered stripping more limited protections from the area that President Clinton had declared a coral reef ecosystem reserve. It was a sharp departure from "business as usual" for a White House that had pushed to privatize federal land for logging and has designated less wilderness than most presidents over the last forty years."

And with the stroke of a pen, George W. Bush created the single largest act of conservation in U.S. history.

Yes, a TV show made a difference, AGAIN. Now, if the White House residents and staff would only screen *An Inconvenient Truth*! Or the documentary *Freedom to Fascism*, and the Michael Moore exposé of health care in America—or as producer Morgan Spurlock refers to our system, "sick care." As of this writing, these shows are not yet on the White House schedule, but the author remains cautiously optimistic.

The fact that a single documentary—Cousteau's, Gore's, Moore's, Schecter's, Russo's, Greenwald's and others—could have such significant impact (remember the Emmett Till case?) speaks to the power of media. It's almost enough to inspire hope in other areas. However, the level of toxicity between some religious groups and scientific communities needs to be addressed. The fact that a school board in Kansas had to be replaced via an election in order for teachers to be allowed to teach evolution again demonstrates just how destructive that environment is.

America is falling way behind the rest of the world in producing scientists, largely because education programs in this country have undergone such tremendous budget cuts. In addition, many science teachers have to provide their own materials and resources for classroom use.

Only science is going to offer a solution to the global energy problem. Representative Jay Inslee (D-WA) has suggested applying America's enthusiasm and expertise to creating innovative energy programs, such as a new Apollo Project.

New power resources, such as using underwater tidal currents, are on the horizon. Waves of them.

We need to point out to our children that a lot of people have ideas about energy, *but big business has quite another take. After all, the main priority of some energy corporations is their own survival*.

In the past year, coal companies have begun revamping their image to be perceived as a clean, green biz. They are using children on TV, narrating this new "vision," to make the pitch. This, despite the highest rate of fatalities in years among coal miners and reputable, irrefutable scientific information on how clean coal **isn't.**

This goes right along with the recent push for ethanol as a substitute for our dwindling supply of fossil fuel. What those lovely promos do not tell you, the audience, is that it's anything but an "inexpensive," safe alternative fuel, especially in terms of the amount of land needed to grow the crop. It may be a short-term step in a perceived better direction, but there are other, more Earth-friendly options. And, folks, we're not talking about nukes here, either. Run, do not walk to your video store and *see **Who Killed the Electric Car?**!*

A friend of mine has a cartoon — might be an old cartoon from *The New Yorker* — and this little girl is asked, 'Do you know where electricity comes from?' And she points at a power pole saying, 'Electrici-trees!'"
Jeff Goodell, author of *Big Coal: The Dirty Secret Behind America's Energy Future,* as quoted in the environmental e-zine, *Grist*

One way of literally driving home some environmental factoids is to acknowledge pollution caused by shipping and packaging.

In a piece by Chad Heeter called *Fossil Fuel for Breakfast,* published in April 2006 (**www.tomdispatch.com**) you'll find a lesson about your kids' cereal that no commercial will ever cover. Heeter, a former science teacher, notes "Thanks to the global industries that produce, package, and ship our food, each meal you eat also feeds the nation's oil addiction." As Heeter writes:

It's a healthy looking little meal—a bowl of imported McCann's Irish Oatmeal topped with Cascadian Farms organic frozen raspberries, and a cup of Peet's Fair Trade Blend coffee. Like most of us, I prepare my breakfast at home, and the ingredients for this one probably cost me about $1.25. If I went to a café in downtown Berkeley, I'd likely have to add another $6, plus tip, for the same.

My breakfast fuels me up with about 400 calories, and it satisfies me. So, for just over a buck and a half, and a half an hour reading my morning paper in my own kitchen, I'm energized for the next few hours. But before I put spoon to cereal, what if I consider this bowl of oatmeal porridge (to which I have just added a little butter, milk, and a shake of salt) from a different perspective? Say, a Saudi Arabian one?

Then, what you'd be likely to see—what's hidden from our view (not to mention our taste buds) is about four ounces of crude oil.

Throw in those luscious red raspberries and that cup of java (another three ounces of crude) and don't forget those modest additions of butter, milk and salt (another ounce) and you've got a tiny bit of the Middle East, right here in my kitchen.

Now, let's drill a little deeper into this breakfast. Just where does this tiny gusher of oil actually come from? (We'll let this oil represent all fossil fuels in my breakfast, including natural gas and coal.)

Nearly 20 percent of this oil went into growing my raspberries on Chilean farms, many thousands of miles away; those oats in the fields of County Kildare, Ireland, and that specially-raised coffee in Guatemala—think tractors, as well as petroleum-based fertilizers and pesticides.

The next 40 percent of my breakfast fossil fuel equation is burned up between the fields and my local grocery store in processing, packaging and shipping.

Take that box of McCann's oatmeal. On it is an inviting image of pure, healthy goodness—a bowl of porridge, topped by two peach slices.

In that cover picture, scattered around the bowl, are a handful of raw oats, four acorns, and three fresh raspberries. Those raw oats are a reminder that the flakes require a few steps between field and box. In fact, a visit to McCann's Web site illustrates each step in the cleaning, steaming, hulling, cutting and rolling that turns the raw oats into edible flakes. Those five essential steps require significant energy costs.

Next, my oat flakes go into a plastic bag (made from oil) which is, in turn, inserted into an energy-intensive, pressed wood-pulp printed paper box. Only then does my "breakfast" leave Ireland and travel over five thousand fuel-gorging, CO2-emitting miles by ship and truck to my grocery store in California.

Coming from another hemisphere, my raspberries take an even longer fossil-fueled journey to my neighborhood. Though pack-aged in a plastic bag labeled Cascadian Farms (which hints that they are from the good old Cascade Mountains of Washington State, not so far away) the small print on the back, stamped "Prod-uct of Chile" tells it all—and what it speaks of is a 5,800 mile journey to northern California.

If you've been adding up percentages along the way, perhaps you've noticed that a few tablespoons of crude oil in my bowl have not been accounted for. That final 40 percent of the fossil fuel in my breakfast is used up by the simple acts of keeping food fresh and then preparing it. In home kitchens and restau-rants, the chilling in refrigerators and the cooking on stoves us-ing electricity or natural gas, gobbles up more energy than you might imagine.

For decades, scientists have calculated how much fossil fuel goes into our food by measuring the amount of energy consumed in growing, packing, shipping, consuming, and finally, disposing of it. The "caloric input" of fossil fuel is then compared to the energy available in the edible product, the "caloric output."

What they've discovered is astonishing. According to research-ers at the University of Michigan's Center for Sustainable Agri-culture, an average of over 7 calories of fossil fuel is burned up for every calorie of energy we get from our food.

This means that in eating my 400 calorie breakfast, I have "consumed" 2,800 calories of fossil fuel energy. Some researchers say the ratio may be as high as 10 to 1.

But this is only an average. My cup of coffee gives me only a few calories of energy, but to process just one pound of coffee requires over 8,000 calories of fossil fuel energy—*the equivalent of a quart of crude oil, thirty cubic feet of natural gas, or two and a half pounds of coal.*

…What appeared to be a simple, healthy meal of oatmeal, raspberries and coffee looks different now. By the end of a week, I've eaten the equivalent of over two quarts of Valvoline. And what about the mornings I head to Denny's for a Grand Slam breakfast of eggs, pancakes, bacon and sausage?

What I eat for breakfast connects me to the planet, deep into its past with the fossilized remains of plants and animals which are now fuel—as well as into the future, when these nonrenewable resources will likely be in scant supply. Maybe these thoughts are too grand to be having over breakfast, **but I'm not the only one on the planet eating this morning.**

My meal traveled thousand of miles around the world to reach my plate. But then there's the rise of 600 million middle class people of India and China. They're already demanding the convenience of packaged meals and foreign flavors. What happens when middle class families of Indians and Chinese decide they want Irish oats for breakfast, topped with organic raspberries from Chile? They'll dip more and more into the communal oil well.

And someday soon, we'll all suck it dry.

Teach your kids about the importance of how we live our lives.

Sustainability and greenthink are already **energetically** embraced by kids.

Shouldn't we listen to how they talk about the planet we are leaving in their hands? They deserve much better than an environmental forecast that reads:

CLOUDY, WITH A CHANCE OF CHAOS

(The author did not invent this phrase, but uses it all the time— it's the terrific title of Eugene Linden's January 2006 climate change article in *FORTUNE* magazine.)

ZAP

1. Do the breakfast lesson with your kids, figuring out what came from where, and how far it traveled to get to your table. Buying locally grown foods is a great start—especially food that is not commercially packaged. Tell your kids that in addition to looking at healthy content and costs, you're also going to see how many miles per gallon the stuff in that shopping cart is really getting.

2. Help your kids create a video library on science topics by recording high-interest specials such as hurricane safety, fire prevention, and rapid climate change. Include PBS's *Nova*, the Discovery Channel, the Learning Channel, and that universal kid (and adult) fave, Animal Planet. (Parents who have mastered the art of recording can have a backlog of gems for when you hear that phrase "But there's nothing *on*.") By the way, The Discovery Channel's 2006 season will feature reports from Ted Koppel (who may even end up with a Web-cam—a "TedCam"—in his home) and other topnotch journalists. Reread the first sentence of this paragraph, and check them out!

3. Some of the best experiences in "enhanced viewing" take place during science programming—encourage your kids to go online to the show's Web site *during the show*. This is especially true for the programs about exploring the pyramids, how tsunamis form, and recent specials on the climate change crisis. Try it. (It helps to hit PAUSE as you dash to the computer.)

History and science, blended, make a great shake—especially in well-done recreations of global events like *Krakatoa*. "Documentary" is no longer synonymous with "boring." Check one out at your library (where they're usually free) or video store. Don't forget to thank the proprietor and the librarian.

While you're at the library, look for *Gone Tomorrow: The Hidden Life of Garbage*, by Heather Rogers (New Press, 2005.) She'll "guide you through the grisly, oddly fascinating world of trash, from garbage can to landfill." It's part exposé, part social commentary, and after you share some of her ideas with your family, you'll never look at garbage quite the same way again.

You'll really try to create less of it. Ditto for *Made To Break*, by Giles Slade, about our disposable culture.

The Sundance Channel has launched a new effort, *Sundance Green*, which will feature environmental programming. Sundance not only offers outstanding works by new, diverse faces and voices, but also brought Air America by TV to listeners who could not yet listen on the radio.

Thanks, Robert Redford!

And after you finish this chapter, take a tip from a recent show on *Oprah*: Ask your kids how many incandescent light bulbs they want to replace every month with the more energy efficient kind, until all the lights in your home are Smart Bulbs. Every step counts. Your kids may think their parents are pretty smart bulbs, too.

Thanks to Tom Engelhardt of **www.tomdispatch.com** for immeasurable energy and inspiration and Chad Heeter for changing forever the way we look at food.

PAUSE

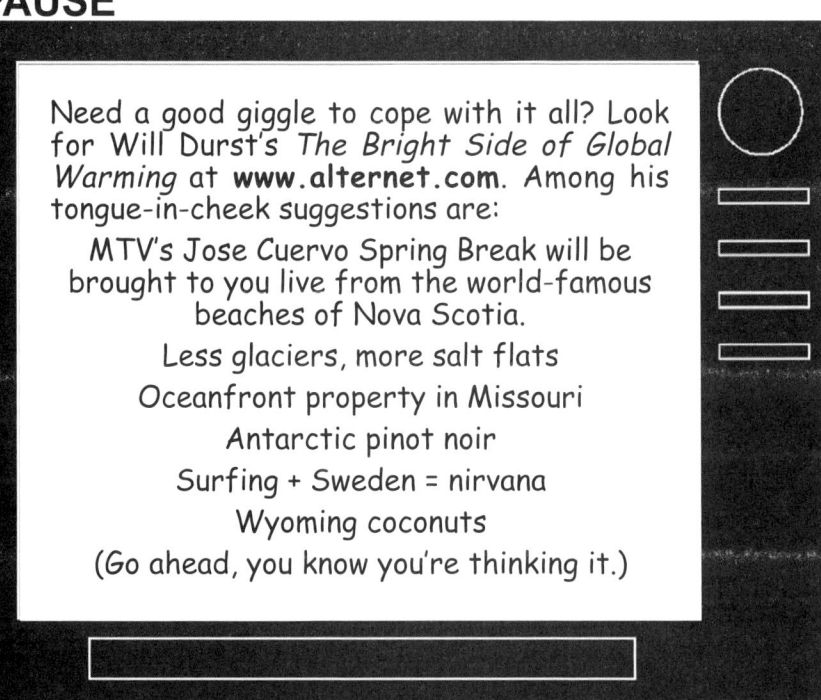

Need a good giggle to cope with it all? Look for Will Durst's *The Bright Side of Global Warming* at **www.alternet.com**. Among his tongue-in-cheek suggestions are:

MTV's Jose Cuervo Spring Break will be brought to you live from the world-famous beaches of Nova Scotia.

Less glaciers, more salt flats

Oceanfront property in Missouri

Antarctic pinot noir

Surfing + Sweden = nirvana

Wyoming coconuts

(Go ahead, you know you're thinking it.)

The best thing about TV is that you can find a show on just about any interest that any kid would have on TV. The worst thing about TV is when your parents don't let you watch certain things.

Spencer, grade 6

Power

Super

Chanel up

Volum up

Call frend

Chanel down

Volum down

Some thing ro drink

tack trasour

detroy enimys

bring game boy

Clean room

food

misels
O O O O O O O

bomes
O O O O O O O

do home Work

Sleep ray

get Art uticls

Confus ray

Unsigned

AUX

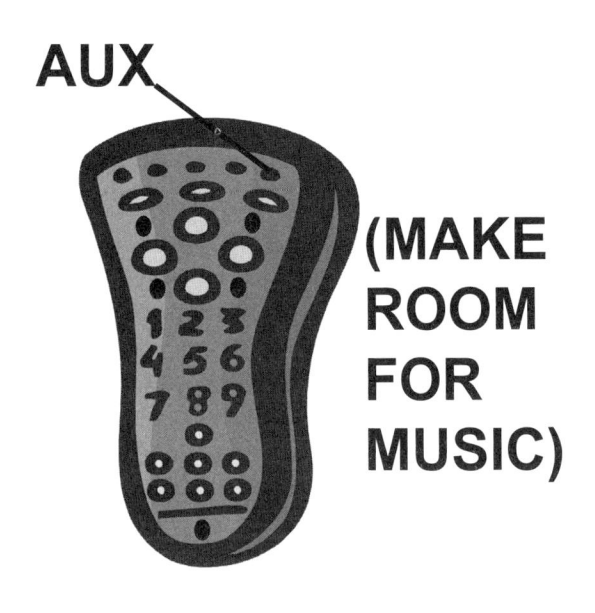

(MAKE ROOM FOR MUSIC)

Granted, the thing in the living room is a whole lot bigger than an iPod or MP3. But good things CAN come in large packages.

That news-spewing, "Idol"-creating, monster-truck raging, sportscasting, house-renovating, clutter-clearing, jewelry-hawking, wildlife-documenting, cartoon-sketching, mystery-solving, talk-show-confessing, sermon-giving, gavel-pounding, newscasting, rock 'n' rolling thing in the living room has an often overlooked capability.

It's a music box.

All you need to do to explore a wide variety of music is to pick a three-digit number in the music section of your cable or dish lineup (usually the 900s) and go for it. This will be more fun if you don't look at the guide first.

But if you must, be assured that from "big-haired rock" to Broadway, you are bound to find something you like.

Keep in mind that these are not music videos—you still have to go to MTV2 and VH1 for those. This is music only.

And sometimes, that's all you need. As Shakespeare said, "If music be the food of life....PLAY ON!"

ZAP

1. Remember the song "Dancin' in the Streets" by Martha and the Vandellas? Well, Martha Reeves is still singing, but in January 2006 she became a city council member in her home town, Detroit. She is working hard to make sure that music programs in public schools continue to thrive. Is there still a music program in your children's school? If there is, celebrate and support it by offering to help with a fundraiser. If there isn't, <u>run, do not walk, to your next school board meeting, and work to get it back.</u>

2. Go with your child and some friends to a live concert of his or her choosing. After you recover your hearing, look for a CD or a concert DVD of that group (or a live appearance on a music channel) and enjoy the experience all over again. You may find *yourself* looking for the new CD before they do—as the author did after her family's experience with an all-Canada lineup of GOB, Simple Plan, and Avril LaVigne. Then check the TV schedules for upcoming broadcast appearances.

3. Consider an upgrade to "surround sound" or new speakers. The difference in your viewing experience (not just music, but everything else, too!) will astound you.

Music .... MTV. Hip hop Countdown

Caitlin

TIMER

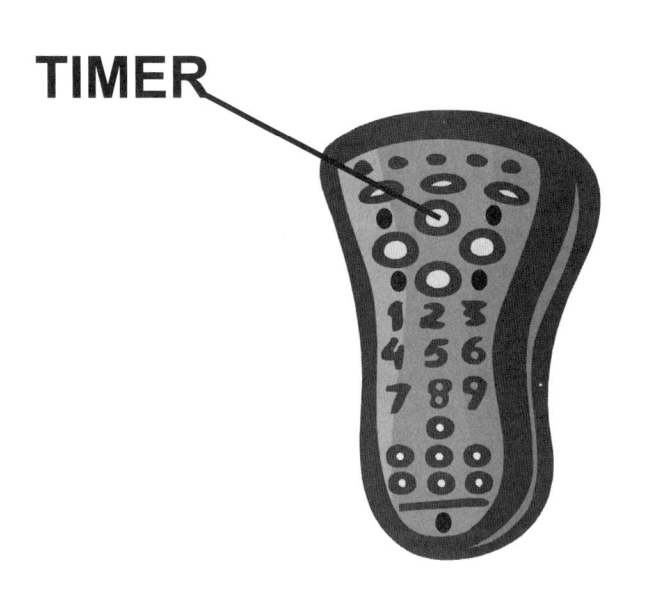

According to the most recent statistics, children in the United States watch about twenty-eight hours of television a week, a statistic certain to be revised upward when the next studies are released. But that varies from home to home and family to family. If your kids come home from school and turn on the TV while they do their homework, and then leave it on and watch once the school stuff is done, **they are developing an addiction to video wallpaper, and it's a hard habit to break.**

Managing screen time is sometimes harder for adults than for kids, but we all need to make the attempt.

I watch TV because it keeps me occupied. Caitlin, grade 6

I watch TV because, most of the time, I'm bored. Nicole, grade 6

ZAP 1. Remember what this button is called. THEN GET ONE. The only way your kids will believe how much TV they are really watching is to use a TIMER and document it.

2. Have one of the kids set up a graph showing how many hours EACH family member watches per week. The more detail, the better. This can be expanded to other graphics done on computer, or pie graphs on paper plates, showing how many family members watch news, for instance, or how many hours of cartoons/animation are watched per week. MAKE IT FUN. And be sure to place the finished project somewhere near the TV, PROMINENTLY DISPLAYED!

3. Having a timer go off when it's someone else's turn to make a viewing decision means the parent is not the "heavy." The TIMER just told the child that his/her time was up, not the evil sibling(s), boring parents, annoying guy who's going out with the older sister, or the sports jock who feels obligated to commandeer the remote for the big game. The TIMER is dispassionate and objective. It will not react to weaseling, whining, and guilt trips. And it makes more sense for a timer to go off than an angry family member.

The best thing about TV is that you can get away from your brothers/sisters.
Emily, grade 3

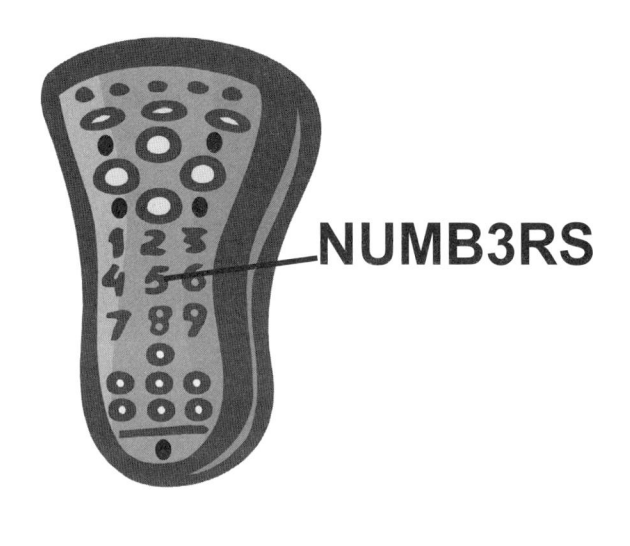

NUMB3RS

This chapter is **not** about the show **NUMB3RS**, which the author happens to like. It's a good show for its premise alone: that we can do a whole lot more than homework (or taxes) with digits. (The cast, which features the talents of several gifted, mostly white male actors, does, however, need some work in the area of diversity.)

Still, in a world where surveillance, FBI, identity theft, and crime-solving are terms with which most households are somewhat familiar, there are some compelling plot lines. (And don't say your kids can't see it because it's on at 10 p.m. When it goes into syndication, they'll be able to tune in for an afternoon rerun—**just as they're doing their math homework**.)

So the first numbers we can look at are expressions of time. Well, in the words of any *Sopranos* knockoff: "***Fugghedaboudit***." With DVR, VOD, and podcasts, we can record and download what we want to see and view it whenever we want to see it. Time slots are going the way of the dinosaur.

The numbers in this chapter can be divided into two subject areas: ratings and stats.

RATINGS

You've known all along that TV is a numbers game. Stations running programs with the highest numbers of viewers (as monitored during ratings periods, or "sweeps") could charge more for commercial time when those shows aired. The TV stations were happy. The sponsors of the show might not have liked paying higher and higher rates, but the more people who watched the "hit" show, the more potential customers they were able to reach. So the sponsors were happy. The writers, actors, producers, and production staff had steady work because the program was renewed for another year on the network schedule. They were happy. The TV-related businesses thrived, because the show had GREAT RATINGS.

So how do ratings work?

The RATING is the average number of people watching for every minute the program aired. It can appear as a whole number or a percentage. So imagine that your favorite (fictitious) program, *Yes, My Mom Is a Diva,* has a rating of ten thousand. That means, on the average, 100,000 pairs of eyeballs (or, 200,000 eyeballs) were watching that show **each minute.**

The ratings firm most people are familiar with is Nielsen's. They take a sampling of viewer choices, recording what a household watches, using a small box that monitors changes of channels and length of time programs are watched.

According to *Ad Age* magazine's Claire Atkinson, Nielsen provides three streams of ratings data:

People who watch shows LIVE

People who watch shows in playback via DVRs the same day (called "LIVE + same day")

People who watch shows via playback a week later (called "LIVE+7 Days")

But people who buy advertising time are concerned that when people view a show via playback, they may skip the commercials that cost so much to put on the air in the first place.

So advertisers are striking back:

1. There is a lot of encouragement in technological circles to create DVRs that cannot skip the commercials.

2. Product placement within the body of a program is increasing in two major ways: First, the product, with its label toward the camera, will be prominently displayed *(American Idol, Extreme Home Makeover.)* Second, as you now know, much to the chagrin of television writers and the TV Writer's Guild, the actual names of products are being written into dialogue as the plot of a program moves forward. You can expect to read more about this in coming seasons.

In the fall of 2006, there was an earthquake in the TV ratings scenario. For the first time in TV history, the Nielsens are going to rate commercials—not individual ones (YET!)—but how many are actually watched between show segments. In the 2006-2007 season, Nielsen will compute an "average commercial rating" for each program. ***If advertisers start buying TV time based on commercial ratings, networks will have a greater incentive to keep viewers tuned in during breaks.***

Mike Lotito, CEO of Media IQ, which studies the effect of commercial clutter on viewers, has a basic analysis: There is a "direct correlation" between the number of commercials in a break (also called a "pod") and the number of viewers who stay tuned during that break. Lotito was quoted in *Ad Age* as saying, "The greater number of messages in a pod, the greater chance the consumer will leave it. We are bored by commercials." Well, DUH.

So how will the new system change the way you watch (or don't watch) commercials? Some shows will begin highlighting upcoming programming during the show, rather than in a separate promo. The new *CW* network, using its own initials, will call commercials "Content Wraps," (CWs) which are actually "mini-shows featuring advertiser brands that stretch across multiple ad breaks," according to *Ad Age*. Some networks, like E! and Style, might add single spot breaks, freezing the programming **so that it jumps directly and unexpectedly into a commercial break.**

It looks as if you can kiss that transitional, polite "And now, a word from our sponsor" phrase bye, bye, bye—so that there's more time to convince you to **buy, buy, buy**.

The SHARE will always be a percentage. Share is the proportion of viewers watching a specific program out of all the people watching TV at the particular time the show aired.

So, let's say *Yes, My Mom Is a Diva* airs every night from 7 to 8 p.m. (the time when moms feel least like the divas we are, because kids are being put into a bath, or to bed, or they are doing homework, or they have just sprung the science project on you and it is due tomorrow, and there is a school play and the costume you promised to make is needed by curtain time the next afternoon, and the Save The Salamander Bake Sale cupcakes are still in the Betty Crocker box, and your teenager has just phoned about a slight fender-bender with the family car, and your pet—substitute your family's animals: hedgehog, cat, dog, wombat—has just given birth in your closet, near your best shoes.) For starters.

Well, when you read that *YMMIAD* did really well last night and had a 30 percent share, that means that out of all the households with TV sets on, a third of them were tuned in to *Diva*. In other words, one out of three TVs between 7 and 8 p.m (known in the author's house as "the arsenic hour") were tuned to the channel showing *Diva*.

So now when you read a TV column or entertainment magazine, you'll know exactly what those cryptic numbers really mean, and perhaps that will assist you in understanding how a show you detest gets renewed for another season, while an excellent (but obscure one with only a niche audience) does not.

(Thanks to **www.tvratingsblog.seo-blog.org** for numerical inspiration.)

Was that too complicated? Here is a simpler version:

NUMB3RS MEAN EYEBALLS.

Eyeballs make money for TV in two ways:

First, eyeballs are seeing new products that audience members (yes, your family) can nag for and buy.

Second, eyeballs on a certain show make money for the TV stations, who can charge the advertisers for all that exposure…to all those eyeballs.

PAUSE

STATS

This portion of the chapter is right where it's supposed to be—near the end of the book, so you can easily find it.

TV statistics are in a constant state of flux. Remember the "flux ca-pacitor" from that *Back to the Future* trilogy? Well, new statistics are being produced every day by futuristic statistical "machinery" in aca-demic, public relations, consumer, political, military, and even religious circles.

But keep in mind that, according to author Julie Dobrow, "Even the phrasing of the questions can influence a study's outcome."

To become media savvy readers of statistics, she suggests that we need to ask these kinds of questions:

How is the research presented in the press?

How was the research conducted?

Who made up the sample, and how were they selected?

Who conducted the research?

Who funded the research?

Who stands to gain from the way the numbers are presented?

The Center for Media Literacy (CML) reminds us that "children are often 'counted' in assessments of television viewing hours, such as Nielsen ratings, if they were simply present in the room while the TV was on."

So take every TV stat with the proverbial grain of sea-salt.

The Scariest Stat of All (2005):

You are more likely to find a home with two TVs than two parents.

Here are some reliable statistics about children and TV, pulled from trusted sources and well-documented research. By the time this book reaches your hands, there will be many more "NUMB3RS" available, so read these, and then go out and find your own.

From University of Michigan Health Systems:

In a typical American home, the TV is on seven to eight hours a day.

The average child spends more time per week watching TV than in school. Or sleeping.

By age seventy, the average TV viewer will have watched seven to ten *years* of TV.

When nonwhites are shown on TV, they are mostly stereotyped, and many children accept those stereotypes because of repetition on-air—not to mention reruns.

In a study of 1555 elementary school children, white kids who watched more violent TV programming said that they believed that African American kids were less competent and *less obedient*. (Author's italics)

Women on TV tend to be in positions where they are dominated by men.

Kids see one thousand to two thousand TV ads for alcohol each year.

Programs for kids are five to six times more violent than programs for adults:

> In prime-time shows, there are three to five violent acts per hour.

> In Saturday morning children's programming (now available 24/7 on Cartoon Network and other cable outlets) there are twenty to twenty-five violent acts per hour.

> Most violent acts go unpunished on TV, especially in children's programming and are often accompanied by humor. Even "good guys" beating up "bad guys" gives

a message that violence is normal, okay, and a way to solve a disagreement.

TV glamorizes violence. TV seems to promote violence as a fun and effective way of getting what you want.

Watching TV violence leads to more aggressive behavior. (Try to get a kid who has just watched a ninja/kung-fu/cop-show/crime-show/fight scene to sit still for sixty seconds.)

Kids see about ten thousand TV rapes, assaults and murders every year.

The average child will have seen eight thousand homicides by the end of eighth grade.

A seventeen-year-long study found that teenaged boys who watched more than an hour of TV a day were four times as likely to commit acts of violence than those who watched less than an hour a day.

Children imitate the violence that they see.

A group called **Children Now** studied how kids were shown on children's entertainment shows. They found that:

Children on television are most often motivated by peer relationships and romance.

Entertainment TV rarely shows children dealing with important issues.

Most child characters engage in anti-social behaviors that often yield positive results. (Think sit-coms.)

On local TV news:

Almost half of all stories on children (45 percent) focus on crime.

Children account for 25 percent of the population, but only 10 percent of local news stories.

African American children account for 61 percent of all stories involving children of color, followed by Latino children (32 percent.) Asian, Pacific Rim, and Native American children are virtually invisible on local news.

African American boys are more likely than any other group to be portrayed as perpetrators of crime and violence; Caucasian girls are most likely to be shown as victims.

Don't use TV as a reward or punishment—this gives TV **WAY TOO MUCH IMPORTANCE!**

For kids, having a TV in the bedroom is linked to a decline in grades and an increase in sleep problems. Unfortunately, a third of kids aged two to seven, and two-thirds of kids aged eight and up have TVs in their rooms. Besides, if the TV is in their bedroom, you don't know what they're watching.

Check out Ready to Learn programs (PBS) at **www.pbs.org**.

Visit the American Academy of Pediatrics Web site for *The Smart Parent's Guide to Kids' TV*, and *Guia para Ver La Television en Familia*, a Spanish publication from ERIC (the Educational Resources Information Center.)

It may be reassuring to know that children who watch moderate amounts of television also tend to read a lot.
Julie Dobrow

AAP (American Academy of Pediatrics) recommends that parents limit TV viewing to one or two hours a day at most. (Contact them about their excellent media literacy materials at **www.aap.org**.) An alternative plan is to agree to an hour a day during the week, and two to three hours a day on weekends.

And for children under the age of two:

NONE!

From TV-Free America:

According to the Nielsen ratings, the average American watches at least four hours of TV a day—or the equivalent of fifty-two nonstop TV-watching days per year. (1998)

DVD/video rentals every day in the U.S.: six million

Library items checked out every day: three million

Chance that an American falls asleep with the TV on three nights a week: 25 percent.

Americans who say they watch too much TV: 49 percent.

Percentage of Americans who watch TV during dinner: 66

Percentage of Americans who can name the Three Stooges: 59.

Percentage of Americans who can name three Supreme Court Justices: 17.

From GENERATION M: Media Study in the Lives of eight- to eighteen-year-olds, The Kaiser Foundation

According to 51 percent of those polled, TVs are on most of the time.

53 percent of families have no rules at all about TV viewing.

63 percent say the TV is usually on during meals.

From the California Wellness Foundation:

17 percent of all children in America are living in poverty.

33 percent of African American children live in poverty.

29 percent of Latino children live in poverty.

14 percent of white children live in poverty.

10 percent of Asian children live in poverty.

The numbers of Native American, Pacific Rim, and Middle Eastern children living in poverty were not given.

In any group of twenty kids, three of their families are living on food stamps.

(Poverty, hunger, and ignorance are more dangerous to a child's well-being than TV will ever be. LZ)

ZAP

1. Just as parents who are also smart sports fans can figure out how to give kids an interesting math lesson via sports stats, a media-literate parent can use ratings and rankings to play with math too. Use the ratings from *Entertainment Weekly* to track a particular show over an eight-week period. Figure out where the show falls in terms of average number of viewers, and make your own executive decision about whether or not the program will see another season. Then see how accurate your predictions are.

2. As the election cycle approaches, keep track of political ads. You'll be able to tell "by the numbers" which candidate raised more money to get his or her message across. (For one thing, more money means more political ads.) Track them.

3. Create a survey on TV watching with your kids for their friends (and share it with their parents.) At the very least, you'll get confirmation of whether or not (as some kids have claimed) other parents are letting their children watch the X-rated material (cringe, gag) in the "animated reality show" *Drawn Together!*

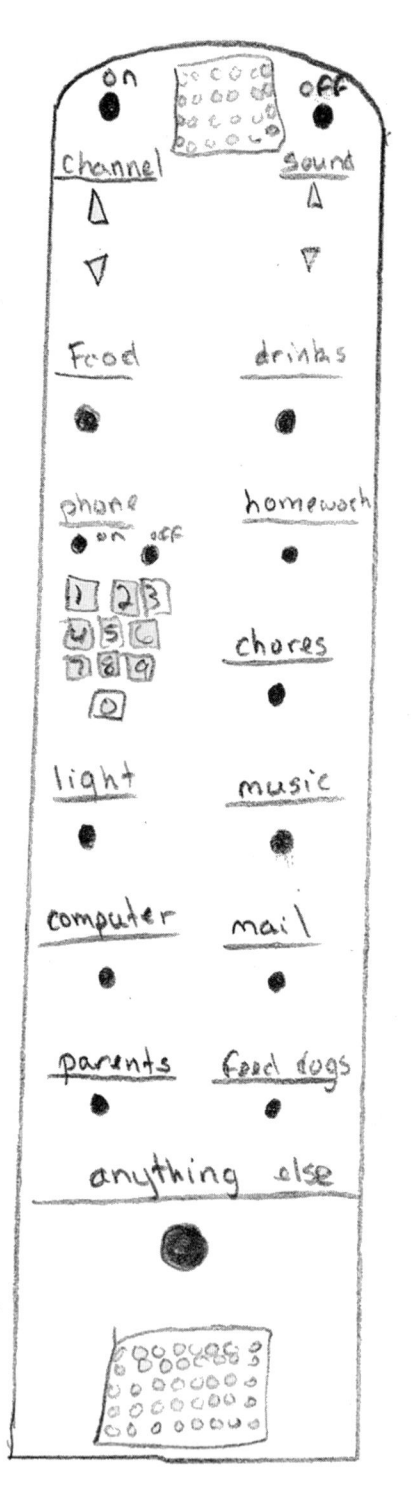

Laura

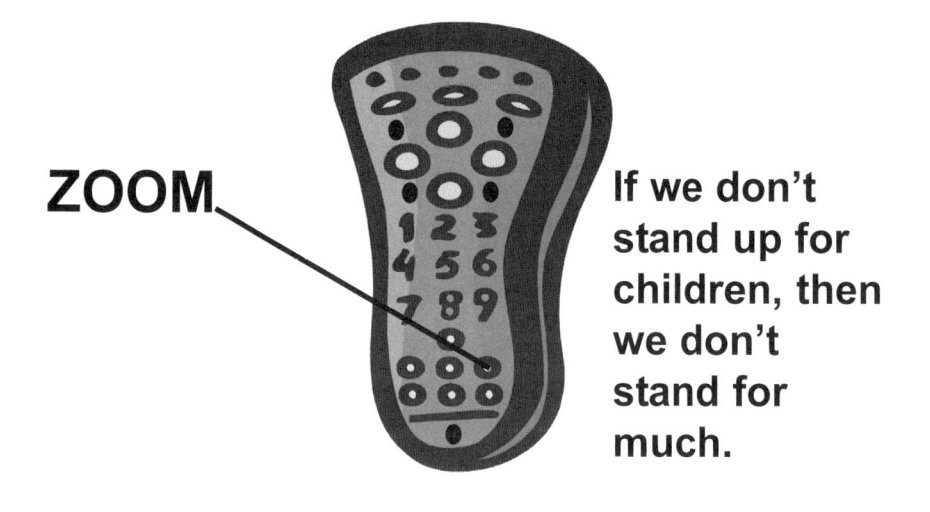

ZOOM

If we don't stand up for children, then we don't stand for much.

"If you don't like the way the world is, you change it. You have an obligation to change it. You just do it one step at a time." Marian Wright Edelman, Founder and President, Children's Defense Fund

Since 1960, when a clean-cut, relaxed, and confident John Kennedy looked over from the podium at his sweating, uncomfortable opponent, then Vice President Richard Nixon, TV has become the center stage upon which the game of politics is played. Nearly half a century later, the media artists who sculpt the daily image of any politician can measure, sometimes within hours of an event, what the price of looking haggard, shouting loudly, stumbling verbally (or physically), or saying what the candidate thought was an off-air comment (when the mic was really on) will be. In close elections, in our videographic society, any blooper could wind up as the lead story **on the next hour's news**.

The governor of California, Arnold Schwarznegger, once starred in a futuristic film about game shows, called *The Running Man*. Put aside for a moment the "fun fact" that, after a career of action movies, he actually became "a running man"—a politician. Let's look at the story.

SPONGEHEADZ: U & MEdia

In the film, the decisions made by the show's fictional host, Richard Dawson, (the real-life host of the original *Family Feud* as in "Good answer, Mom!") were based on ratings that changed minute by minute. If a contestant bombed with the audience, a meter indicated a drop in ratings almost instantly. Ratings were fed back to the show's producers, so that the show could constantly tweak its own content to achieve maximum numbers. When the movie opened, it seemed like a good dig at the Nielsen ratings. Now it seems like a prediction.

By the way, the "edited for TV" version of *The Running Man* has **completely removed the entire ratings story line**—you'll have to rent the original to see it. And maybe, after reading this, you'll want to.

Science fiction has become demographic fact, and nowhere is that more visible than in election years. We are approaching what promises to be the most media-manipulated election cycle in American history.

We need to "zoom in" to the election cycle, that most basic element of democracy, by synthesizing the media literacy lessons of *SPONGEHEADZ: U & MEdia* as they apply to voting.

PLAY - Have fun! Campaign for your candidates and issues as vigorously as you can.

MUTE - Don't sit silently and absorb (like a sponge!) the other side's campaign rhetoric. Speak out, as often as possible!

POWER - Captain Planet said it best: The POWER is YOURS! And once you've voted, offer rides to people who need them.

BALANCE - Monitor the coverage of the results on different local **and** national networks.

COLOR - Look at the crowds at polling places and campaign headquarters. See where the delays are. Watch to see what groups, if any, have insufficient numbers of voting machines or time to use them. Take notes and if you think voters are being disenfranchised, TAKE NAMES, TIMES, AND PRECINCTS. Then call the media.

STEREO(TYPES) - Don't let anyone badmouth another voter for any reason, even if someone takes too long or makes a mistake because s/he is too old, young, or whatever. Teach tolerance, even if the other candidate ends up winning.

SAT - Going "LIVE" will happen frequently—you'll see satellite trucks everywhere. Watch the experienced reporters as well as the newer ones to find out who really *is* on top of the results.

CHANNEL - For your mental health, switch often!

PAGE - Read and analyze the spin in print media the day after the election.

SELECT - Do this wisely. Your SELECTion has consequences.

VOLUME (of) VIOLENCE - Keep the peace.

DISPLAY - Try not to cost your local stations a six-figure fine if your candidate's career ends up "down the tubes." If your side prevails, try to be a tad less joyous than, say, Bono.

EDIT - See who says what when it's all over. Part of the fun of live broadcasting is its spontaneity—and the karmic right of any candidate to put his/her foot in his/her mouth, even on Election Day/Night.

DELETE - your other plans for once. This is truly IMPORTANT. Promise yourself that no matter who wins, you'll work to delete war, famine, ignorance, and fear, starting now.

REV/REW - See what went right or wrong in your candidate's campaign.

FF - What kind of changes will a new face bring? And how fast? *The Iceman Cometh*, and so doth January. Always.

SETUP - If you're an activist, your setup should include some pillows and blankets in the living room. You may be tracking election results for most of the night.

PAUSE - Remember every editorial cartoon that made you cringe or laugh. Then just laugh.

TIMER - It's two years until the next election. Decide how you'll be involved.

SPONGEHEADZ: U & MEdia

CLEAR - We share a planet. Work for the candidate who plans on working to save it. Tomorrow, join an environmental campaign. After all, in a nod to James Carville, "It's the environment, stupid."

AUX - Music is a part of politics, whether "The Eyes of Texas Are Upon You" or you "Don't Stop Thinkin' About Tomorrow." Someone will hear "The Theme from Titanic," but others will be singing "Celebrate!"

STOP - worrying. In two years, you can do this all over again.

NUMB3RS - See whose were correct in the morning.

ON/OFF - No matter what happens, don't get turned off. If your side loses, work harder. If your side wins, work harder to make a better future.

No matter what, there is hard work ahead!

Our Spongeheadz are worth it.

History will record that the greatest tragedy of this period...was not the strident clamor of bad people, but the appalling silence of the good people.
Rev. Martin Luther King

SPEAK UP.
SPEAK OUT.
RECLAIM YOUR AIRWAVES.
THEY BELONG TO YOU—
AND YOUR SPONGEHEADZ.

1. Take your kids with you when you vote. Tell them who you voted for, and why. Mention the things you like about your choice—where s/he stands on the environment, energy, war(s), health care, privacy—as much info as you think they can handle. That gives them a stake, however small, in watching the results come in.

2. If you have friends or neighbors who can't get to a polling place, give them a lift. Your kids need to see how important this process is.

3. No matter who wins, as was mentioned earlier, make an effort to make positive changes. GET INVOLVED, and GET BUSY!

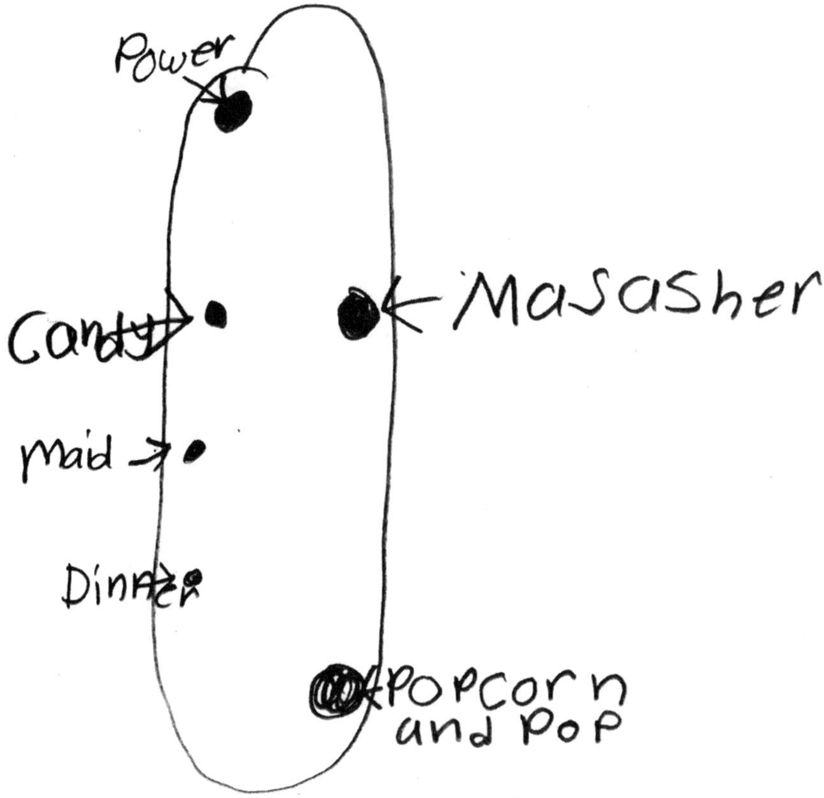

Power

Candy

Maid

Dinner

MaJasher

Popcorn and Pop

Sarah

ON/OFF

The ON/OFF Button Is the Ultimate *ZAP!*

Peggy Charren, founder of Action for Children's Television, has said, "You can always turn off the TV. But you can't turn on what isn't there."

FINALLY:

PUT DOWN THE REMOTE CONTROL.

Get up off the sofa and do what you're supposed to do with any sponge, and all Spongeheadz…..

SQUEEZE

THEM!

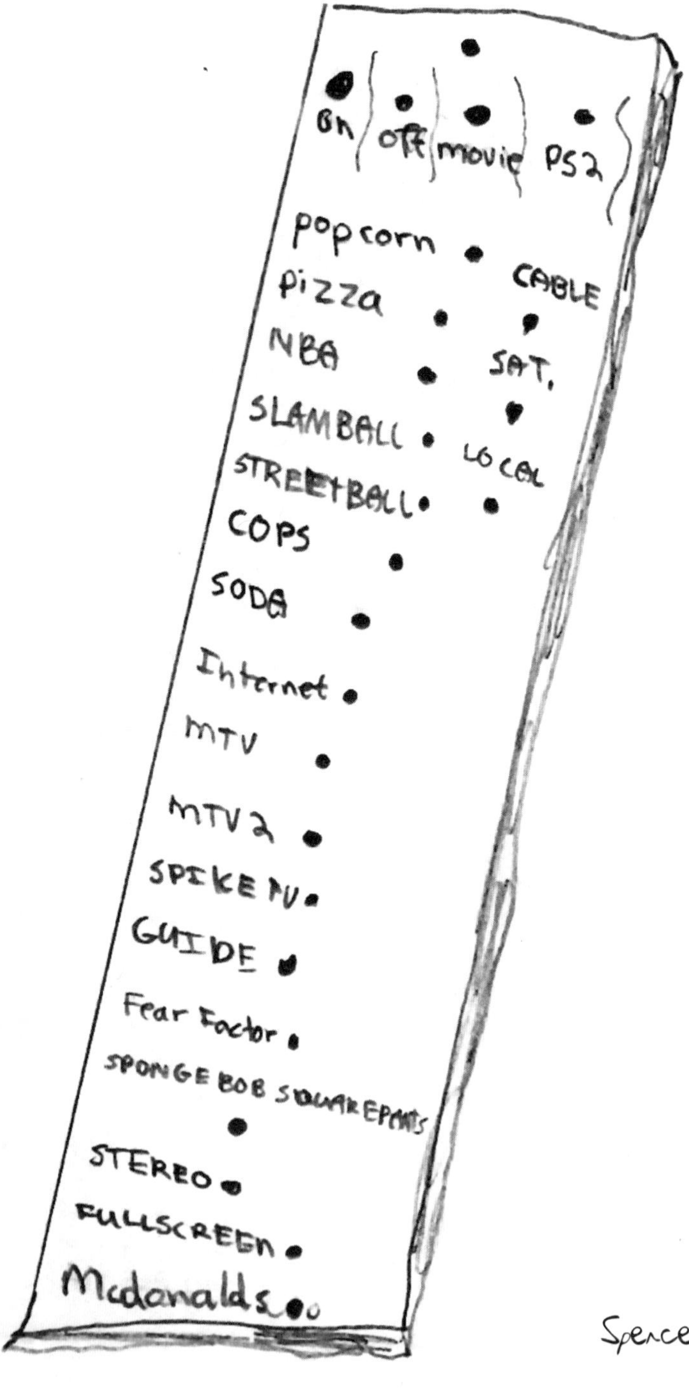

On Off movie PS2

popcorn •   CABLE

pizza   •

NBA   •   SAT,

SLAMBALL •   LOCAL

STREETBALL • •

COPS   •

SODA   •

Internet •

MTV   •

MTV 2   •

SPIKE TV •

GUIDE •

Fear Factor •

SPONGE BOB SQUAREPANTS
       •

STEREO •

FULLSCREEN •

Mcdonalds ••

Spencer

CONCLUSION: "PROGRAM" AND "GUIDE" ARE ALSO VERBS

Even If you were asked, you wouldn't let complete strangers walk into your homes and advise your kids on how to eat, how to dress, and how to think. So why are you letting TV do it?

There are few more powerful forces in your child's life than media. But…

NEWSFLASH: The most powerful and important one is… U!

(Yes, you!)

SPONGEHEADZ: U & MEdia

Parents are the U and the ME in *SPONGEHEADZ: U & MEdia*. Sometimes, U can clarify the ideas in this book for your kids. Other times, parents will be the ME, letting your kids explain to you why they think what they do about TV.

Time with our kids is melting faster than our glaciers or "the snows of Kilimanjaro." Use the precious bit of it that you have to talk **with** your kids (not at them) and to open a dialogue. TV may be their window on the world, but you need to be there to keep the view clear, to let in fresh air and the winds of change. Stay tuned.

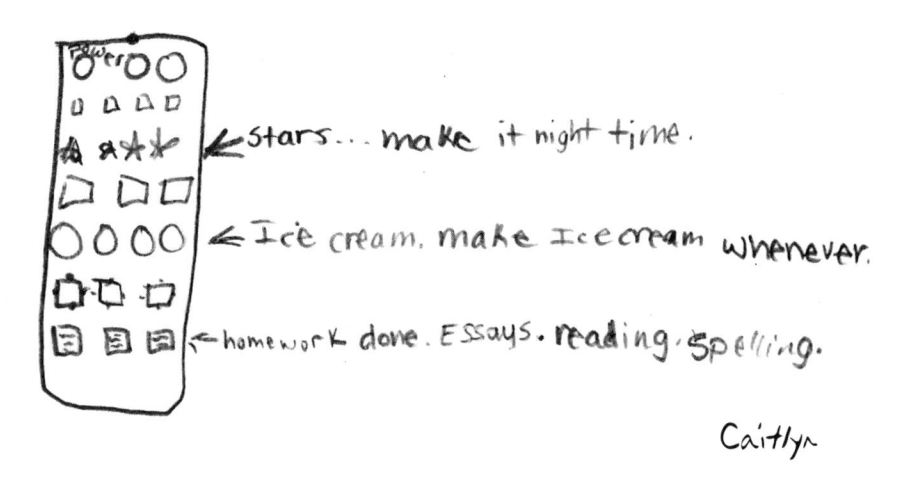

← Stars... make it night time.

← Ice cream. make Ice cream whenever.

← homework done. Essays. reading. spelling.

Caitlyn

RESOURCES

This is a partial list of resources, and even these "best of the best" are being updated hourly. So use this list as a starting point, and if you find a great resource that's not listed here, e-mail me at **lynnztv @earthlink.net**. Your suggestion may go in a future edition of *SPONGEHEADZ: U & MEdia*.

Organizations/Web Sites

About Face **www.about-face.org**

> This Web site was created to combat negative and unrealistic images in media. It offers a Gallery of Offenders, but even better, a positive Image Gallery.

Action for Media Education (AME) **www.action4mediaeducation.org**

> This outstanding group has led the Pacific Northwest and the nation in innovative media approaches for students, kids, parents and teachers.

Action Coalition for Media Education (ACME) **www.acmecoalition.org**

> ACME is a true coalition of progressive media activism and includes organizations such as Free Press and CCFC. Outstanding!

AdBusters/Media Foundation **www.adbusters.org**

> Based in Vancouver, B.C., Canada, AdBusters examines the impact of media on society. Their anti-ads and uncommercials are FAMOUS. Check out their magazine!

Adflip **www.adflip.com**

> Check out this huge database of print ads dating back to the 1940s, including early tobacco ads (when cigarettes were good for you—remember?). Teachers, the advertisements can be printed.

Alliance for a Media Literate America (AMLA) **www.amlainfo.org**

> AMLA promotes the application of literacy skills to media and technology messages. A coalition of educators, faith-based groups, health care providers, and consumer advocates, it offers good resources for parents and teachers.

Campaign for a Commercial-Free Childhood
www.commercialfreechildhood.org

> These powerful advocates from the Judge Baker Children's Center and Harvard fight to stop exploitation of and marketing to our kids. Become a member now.

Center for Creative Voices In Media **www.creativevoices.us**

> Creative Voices champions original, independent, and diverse voices in America's media. It strives to educate not only the creative community, but legislators, regulators and the public about critical media issues. A must-see site for those who promote freedom and diversity.

Center for Digital Democracy www.democraticmedia.org

CDD is committed to preserving the openness and diversity of the Internet and encourages noncommercial, public interest programming. Its founder, Jeff Chester is a multi-talented activist/filmmaker/investigative journalist/psychiatric social worker/producer—and visionary. Want to see where media is going? Visit this site for a road map.

Center for Media and Democracy www.prwatch.org

Sheldon Rampton and John Stauber publish PR Watch, a progressive quarterly that questions corporate propaganda and exposes spin. Their new book, *The Best War Ever,* is probably headed to the *New York Times* best-seller list, along with their previous works, including *Toxic Sludge Is Good for You, Weapons of Mass Deception* and *Trust Us, We're Experts!*

Center for Media Literacy www.centerformedialiteracy.org

Books, videos, and curricula for teaching media literacy.

Center for a New American Dream www.newdream.org

A resource for greener living, including smart, environmentally safe school supplies.

Center for Public Integrity www.publicintegrity.org

Nonprofit, nonpartisan "watchdog in the corridors of power."

Centers for Science in the Public Interest www.cspinet.org

Their *Nutrition Action* offers smart, healthy eating tips for kids, as well as other helpful info for parents and teachers. Parents: Check out "Good Cup, Bad Cup: Survival in Latte-Land."

Children and the Media www.childrennow.org

A national organization for people who want children to be the top national public policy priority. Terrific!

Commercial Alert **www.commercialalert.org**

"Protecting Communities From Consumerism," CA works on keeping your smallest consumers from being targeted by marketers.

Committee for Children **www.cfchildren.org**

An outstanding international nonprofit that offers educational programs to seven million children in twenty-one countries. Their goal: "safe children thriving in a peaceful world."

Currents of Awareness **www.COAnews.org**

COA offers connections to many independent news resources, particularly for environmental stories.

Fairness and Accuracy in Reporting **www.fair.org**

The latest truth on the latest truthiness.

Free Press **www.freepress.net**

This nonpartisan organization is working to make media reform a reality. It promotes diverse and independent media ownership and universal, affordable access to communications. Who else could get an FCC commissioner onstage with a rock legend, wailing away on a harp? Free Press ROCKS.

Media Awareness Network **www.media-awareness.ca**

MNet is an Ontario-based treasure for "media and information literacy." Their excellent info on helping kids cope with traumatic news coverage is a great help to parents anywhere on this blue marble.

Media Channel **www.mediachannel.org**

The "global network for democratic media" (small d) offers outstanding articles as well as "Important News You May Have Missed," as well as links to AllAfrica Global Media, the largest electronic distributor of African news and info worldwide.

Media Education Foundation **www.mediaed.org**

A tremendous resource for videos, lesson plans, study guides, handouts and critical thinking materials. You'll want to digest their entire catalogue.

Media Literacy Clearinghouse **www.frankwbaker.com**

They don't call it the Internet encyclopedia of media literacy for nothing. It is simply excellent.

National Alliance for Media Arts and Culture's Reel Grrls **www.reelgrrls.org**

ReelGrrls is a unique after-school media and technology training program that empowers girls to critique the way they are portrayed in media. Reel Grrls learn video, audio, and Web production skills. Mentored by a network of multi-cultural women media professionals, this organization believes that if women and girls are to achieve equality and advancement—particularly in media-related fields—they must learn media literacy. Their site offers the following: "Only 3 percent of all the cinematographers in Hollywood are women. A woman has never won the Academy Award for Film Directing. Reel Grrls would like to change that." The first one who does may turn out to be a graduate of this internationally acclaimed program.

National Center for Tobacco Free Kids **www.tobaccofreekids.org**

Excellent resource for this important issue. These good people not only exposed the "new" candy-flavored cigs and smokeless (but not cancer-less) tobacco for kids, they also sponsor the annual Kick Butts Day.

New Mexico Media Literacy Project **www.nmmlp.org**

They "cultivate activism and critical thinking"—and offer good resources.

Project Censored **www.projectcensored.org**

This is a collection of things you didn't hear about—but should have. Even Walter Cronkite checks it out, along with their annual Top 25 Censored Stories. (Yes, the 2007 version is out!)

Project Vote Smart **www.vote-smart.org**

A citizens' organization that researches candidates and elected officials in five categories: bios, issues, voting records, campaign finance, and interest group ratings.

AUTHOR'S NOTE: This visit is best followed by a chaser (John Amato's blog Crooks and Liars, **www.crooksandliars.com**) and multiple visits to Comedy Central.com for inspiration and new candidates to research!

Stay Free Magazine **www.stayfreemagazine.org**

This is a monthly, Brooklyn-based magazine that offers media criticism, explores politics, and tweaks American consumer culture (and some of the odd ways they are all combined.) Smart, funny, and worth the trip.

Teen Futures Media Network **www.teenhealthandthemedia.org**, **www.nwmedialiteracy.org**, **www.teenawareresources.org**

Based at the University of Washington, Teen Futures has led the region in teaching media literacy skills with health applications—notably, in smoking prevention, violence prevention, teen pregnancy prevention, and alcohol abuse prevention. See AME.

Truth Campaign **www.thetruth.com**

You've seen their work—they have a habit of grabbing kids' attention on tobacco issues. They are funded by The American Legacy Foundation, a national, independent health organization, which was established after the MSA (Master Settlement Agreement) between state governments and the tobacco industry.

Truthout **www.truthout.org**

There's no simpler way to say this: You'll find everything about everything. Truthout.org's greatest contribution this year—and there are many— may be its making available Keith Olbermann's 9.11.06 commentary, possibly one of the most powerful on-air statements made this century. The only requirements: a brain, a conscience, and a lot of energy, because once you become a regular, you won't tolerate anything but the truth. Outstanding.

UNITE **www.unitehere.org**

A labor organizing site for union and labor issues.

ZILLIONS **www.zillions.org**

This is Consumer Reports .org 4 Kids. It ROCKS!

Yes, another reminder….This is a PARTIAL list. It does not include the Web sites mentioned in the text, like **www.portionteller.com** or **www.howstuffworks.com**. You might want to try reading this book with a highlighter in one hand, and your remote control in the other. Of course, this means you may have to turn pages with your teeth. Or feet. Ask your kids for suggestions, or better, let *them* turn the pages.

THE KIDZ

The author would like to thank the children (of all ages!) of the following nations:

Aleut	Nisqually
Algonquin	Quilleute
Apache	Quinault
Chehalis	Shoalwater Bay
Cheyenne	S'Klallam
Colville	Skokomish
Elwha	Squaxin Island
Hoh	Suquamish
Inupiaq	Tlingit
Lakota	T'Simshian
Lummi	Warm Springs

And indigenous people everywhere.

You taught me more than I could ever teach you, and you are gifts in my life.

The Creator blesses me with your friendship.

All my relations.

ABOUT THE AUTHOR

Lynn Ziegler is an outspoken advocate for quality children's television. Inspired by Peggy Charren (founder of Action for Children's Television), she was urged by Charren herself to start writing about the "good stuff" on TV. "KidzVue," the first column of its kind on the West Coast (and maybe elsewhere), ran for five years in *Seattle's Child*. During that time, Ziegler left her job as a television news writer, and, as an independent producer with small children of her own, created "Nutri-Rap," a public service announcement on children's nutrition. Described as "an MTV-appproach to nutrition," Nutri-Rap featured an African American rapper, somersaulting fruits and veggies, and a rainbow of Northwest children. In addition to being nominated for a number of short film awards, this PSA won two PIXI Awards, a TELLY, and two regional EMMYs.

In 1992, she became the media critic for the Foundation for Family Television (now called action for Media Education), a volunteer position she still holds. As a spokesperson for AME, she has brought national recognition to both the organization and her own work. Since then, she has written weekly print columns on children's TV and family films for a number of Northwest newspapers, anchored several PBS fundraising drives, and appeared on a number of national and regional radio and TV programs. She launched the first family TV column for *Moms Online*, an e-zine that became part of Oxygen

Media. As *MediaMom,* she contributed dozens of pieces about the importance of making smart viewing choices. And one night, as she addressed a large audience, she held up a sponge and said, "See this? This sits on top of your kid's neck. Our kids are SPONGEHEADZ—they absorb everything. So it's in everyone's best interests to look for the best on TV. And contrary to popular belief, there's some great stuff out there." And the idea for this book was born.

Ziegler, a divorced single mom, has three Alaska Native children. For most of the past decade, she has been living, teaching, and writing in Suquamish, Washington, the ancestral home of Chief Seattle. She and her youngest son, Alik Aaglupak Crockett, now live in Kingston, Washington, while sister, Jesse attends the University of Washington and older brother Chris is pursuing a business career in the Seattle area, with an eye on becoming a paramedic or EMT. Adrenaline is hereditary: Their father is former TV news photographer David Crockett, whose award-winning footage of Mt. St. Helens chronicled the eruption on May 18, 1980.

Lynn's is a frequent face and voice in Pacific Northwest media, advocating for programs that "fire the imagination." On-screen diversity is her particular passion. In 2002, she testified before two members of the FCC about the importance to children of "seeing faces like their own" on television and has since met with both commissioners to further that cause.

In 2003, Lynn was elected to the National Board of ACME, the Action Coalition for Media Education. Her blog, ZMEDIA BLOG, is on the ACME Web site, where she co-developed the organization's independent media awards, the MINDY's. ZMEDIABLOG is also available at blogger.com. She is the "proud cyber-parent" of The Orwell Project, an ongoing listing of alternative news sites on the ACME home page. She recently served on the Board of Directors of a community access station, and in 2005, spoke on media issues at Seattle's Rolling Thunder Festival.

She is a member of NATAS (the National Academy for Television Arts and Sciences) and remains active with AME (formerly the Foundation for Family Television) Action for Media Education, a Seattle-based advocacy group that has pioneered media literacy work, both regionally and nationally. The two groups, working together, made Seattle Public Schools one of the first districts in the United States to make media literacy a part of the required curriculum.

She is active with the Campaign for a Commercial-Free Childhood, See Jane, Commercial Alert, Free Press, People for the American Way, and a host of other organizations.

But her first love (after kids, cats, and a dog) is still getting parents and children to look for "good stuff on TV." She is already working on the outline for her next project, "TV's ABZs," a pre-K intro to media literacy. Her Web site will feature a blog where parents can check out news items about children's television, and where she can continue to recommend shows that encourage children to think, imagine, learn, and act—**and to create media of their own.**

A FINAL DEDICATION

A special thank you to the old friend and companion who lived with this book, day in and day out, who watched every TV show with me, and who stayed nearby as each "button" (chapter) was written…until the very last pages.

I hope I become the human being you always believed me to be.

Merci, Mikey! (a.k.a. "the carpet with legs")

Thanks for thirteen years of unconditional love, that thumping, wagging tail, and all those genuine smiles.

GED, Baby Girl.
God, what an **E**XCELLENT **D**OG!